Button Nose

Eileen Brookes

PublishAmerica
Baltimore

ISBN: 1-4241-3219-3
PUBLISHED BY PUBLISHAMERICA, LLLP
www.publishamerica.com
Baltimore

Printed in the United States of America

To my children, Philip, Michael, and Nicola, and
to all my beautiful grandchildren.

DEDICATION:

I dedicate this book to Keith for being patient with me.
To my children, Philip, Michael, and Nicola, and to all my beautiful Grandchildren.
My thanks to Beryl and Dolly for all your help, and to my friends, Eileen, Gill, Brenda, Cathy, and Margaret for keeping me laughing.
Special thoughts to Jean, and for her Mam and Bill, for making me part of their family.
My thanks also to Louise for the kindness that you showed me, when I needed someone to be there for me, and to all my friends and family who are always there for me. Thank you all so much, and God bless.

Table of Contents

1

"Mary! If you don't stop giggling, we'll all have bloody wobbly lines up the backs of our legs."

"I'm sorry Kathy, but I was just thinking, what would that German think if he knew his parachute was keeping your bum warm."

"Well as long as it's not his hands keeping it warm, I'm not bothered. Now hurry up will you or we'll never get out."

"Yes, hurry up or the war'll be over and the Yanks will have all gone home," Clara chimed in. "And make sure you paint my lines straight as well. I don't want wobbly seams."

"OK! OK! Keep your hair on girls. It's not my fault there are no nylons about is it?"

"We never said it was, all we're asking is that you paint the lines straight so that the blokes think we are wearing stockings," Kathy replied.

"Wasn't it good of Mrs. Harris to make us a pair of French knickers each out of that parachute silk?"

"Yes, Clara, I wouldn't fancy jitterbugging in my old flannels, that would put the fella's right off of me. There you go Kathy, that's you done. Come on Clara and I''ll do yours, then you can do mine."

Since the beginning of the war, things had become very scarce and nylons were now non existent, so when girls went out for a night on the town, they had to stand on top of a table so that someone else could pencil a dark line up the backs of their legs, to make them look as though they were wearing stockings. Of course this meant that suspenders were out, which was a real shame, as the sight of them could get a fella going, but beggars can't be choosers, and a dark line was better than nothing at all.

The three girls had come to Leicester to work in one of the factories which was helping to make ammunitions for the war, and they had found lodgings in the home of a very kind lady who looked after them well.

Fridays were the best day of the week because they had the whole weekend in front of them, and they liked nothing better than dancing at the local Palais De Dance. Tonight was no exception and all three of the girls had been to work that day with their hair wrapped up in a scarf to hide the curlers beneath it.

The American G.I.'s had arrived in Britain only a few weeks previously, and as most of the British boys were away fighting, the yanks had given the girls something to look forward to again. After all, you never knew how long life would last. One bomb in the wrong place and you were a gonna! This thought made women live for the moment, and the handsome American's dressed in their smart uniforms were a sight for sore eyes. Women flocked around them as though they were Gods and naturally the Americans thought themselves in Heaven.

Ready now, the girls hurried to catch the tram to take them into town.

"I hope the bloody Germans stay away tonight girls," Clara said to her mates. "Last week, I missed the last waltz with Graham because of the air raid. They could have waited a bit longer 'till the dance was over."

"Yeah! I've still got a bruise on me toe where somebody stuck their heel into it during the rush to get to the shelter." And Mary took off her shoe to show the others who tutted loudly.

Getting off of the tram at the Clock Tower, they had to laugh when the conductor told them.

"Careful what you're up to tonight, young ladies!"

"Don't worry about us, mate!" Mary shouted back to him. "We're always careful. Daren't do anything else with a mother like mine. Skin me alive she would, if I didn't behave me' sen." And they were still laughing as they turned into Humberstone Gate to where the Palais was, which by now already had a long queue to its door. They didn't have to wait too long before the doors were opened and the crowd began to push forwards.

"Hey, wait your bloody hurry, will you?" Mary shouted to the person behind her who was digging her in her back to make her hurry more quickly, but when she turned around she couldn't help laughing. "Oh bloody hell, I might have known it'd be you. How are you, Pauline? Haven't seen you for ages. How's your Ron? Have you heard from him at all?"

"Yeah! He's been moved to France. Mam's right upset. Yer know how she worries, especially as she lost 'er Dad in the last war. I try to tell 'er he'll be alright, an will come 'ome safely, but it don't stop her worrying."

"Ahh! it must be awful for her. You can understand why she worries, can't you?"

Yeah! Cause I can, an' I do feel for 'er. I'm worried meself, but I have to try and keep me spirits up for 'er sake."

"Bloody wars! It's a bloke that starts them, but it's not them that has to do the fighting. They send young lads to do the job for them instead. Bloody men, always ready for a punch up, aren't they?"

"Trouble is, Mary, we still love the buggers, don't we?"

"Yeah! We must be bloody daft." And when Pauline agreed with her, they both burst out laughing, making everyone else turn around to see what was so funny.

The excitement inside the Palais could be easily felt, what with the buzzing of voices, and the girls' toilet full to bursting as everyone tried to get a last look into the mirrors before venturing into the dance hall.

11

One girl was heard to shout at another.

"Hey, be careful will yer. I nearly put me blinking lipstick up me ruddy nose instead of on me mouth."

"Sorry. I didn't do it on purpose. Somebody knocked me into yer."

"Well just be more careful in future."

"Come on, girls, let's hurry out of here before there's an almighty fight," Pauline told her friends, and when they walked into the dance hall, they soon forgot all about the agro that they had just left, because coming into the room was a crowd of American soldiers.

"Look out world, here they come," whispered Kathy.

"Don't worry, we've already seen them," Mary replied. "Seen anyone you fancy yet?"

"Not yet, but the night is young so I won't pick in a hurry. I'll take my time until I've had a chance to weigh them all up."

As the band began to play a waltz, Kathy grabbed hold of Clara and led her onto the dance floor, whilst Pauline and Mary stood on the side to watch. Pauline offered Mary a woodbine cigarette and lit a match to light it for her, but before she got anywhere close to the cigarette she stopped suddenly, and didn't move again until the light of the match had burnt her finger making her drop it, and as she stubbed it with her shoe to make sure it was completely out, Mary began to shout to her.

"Stop messing about Pauline will you? I've been puffing away at this fag waiting for something to happen, and you haven't even attempted to light it. What's got into you?"

"Shh, I've just seen the man of me dreams come in."

"Have you? Where?"

"Over there! Don't keep looking at 'im. Oh my God, 'e's coming over to us."

"Pauline! Have you lost your marbles? Your Mam would bloody kill you if she knew. You know what she thinks about black and white people mixing."

12

"I don't care Mary. 'es lovely. Look at 'is eyes. Couldn't yer just die for them?"

"You probably will when your Mam sees him." But Pauline hadn't heard a word because she was already on the dance floor with the American's arms holding her close to him, and she thought she'd already died and gone to Heaven.

"I haven't seen you here before have I?" He was asking her now, looking down at her face, making her shake with excitement.

"I 'aven't been for a while, because me brother 'as 'ad to go and fight, an' me Mam doesn't like being on 'er own, so I've been staying in with 'er. How long have you been in Leicester?"

"Only three weeks, but I've been to the Palais a few times. It's a nice place you have here. I'm pleased you decided to come tonight."

"Are yer?"

"Sure I am. What's your name?"

"Pauline. What's yours?"

"Donald, but please call me Don."

"Pleased to meet yer Don."

"Likewise Pauline."

Looking into his eyes, Pauline felt that she had never seen anything so beautiful. They reminded her of deep velvet, and the tenderness they generated was awesome. She couldn't say what, but she knew that there was something special about this man. Something that she couldn't explain or had ever felt before. His skin was black as jet, and although her Mam had instilled into her that bloods shouldn't mix, she knew that she was drawn to this man as though she were magnetised. She didn't fall in love easily, and had never believed in love at first sight, yet, how could she explain her feelings for this man? It was almost as though they had met before in a past life, but she didn't believe in that either, so what was it? Pulling her even closer to him, as though reading her thoughts, she began to feel giddy with love for him. Her heart raced, and his breath on her cheek made her feel breathless. They danced without speaking, each feeling the closeness of the others body against their own. Pauline didn't want the dance to end, she could have danced all night long with him and not become bored, but of course it had to, and as Don took her back to her friends, he too was wishing that he could hold onto her for much longer than the dance had permitted.

Clara and Kathy were the first to return to their seats, and Kathy looked around for Pauline.

"Where's Pauline?" she asked Mary.

"Just coming behind you."

Kathy's face dropped when she saw Pauline with the arm of a black man around her waist.

"Blimey! Good job her Mam's not here to see that. She'd have a bloody fit."

"I did try to warn her, but she wouldn't listen to me."

"Oh well, it's only a dance after all. Not much can go wrong with that can it?" Clara butted in to stick up for Pauline.

Mary kept her thoughts to herself, but it was difficult when Pauline danced every dance with the man.

"Pauline?"

"Yes, Don?"

"I was wondering if you could make it to the cinema tomorrow evening. I could pick you up from home if you could."

"Pauline longed to say yes, but it wasn't as easy as that. What if her Mam saw him, she would forbid her to go out, she had to think of an excuse quickly."

"I'd love to go with you. Thanks for askin', but I have some business I need to do in town, so it might be better if I meet you there. Which one was yer thinking of?"

"The Odeon if that's alright with you? I'll meet you about seven thirty if that's OK?"

"That would be great. I'll look forward to it."

Don gave her a squeeze to let her know that he was pleased, and made Pauline tremble again from the thrill of it. Again, when he offered to walk her home after the dance, she made a quick excuse that she'd already promised to walk with the girls, and it wouldn't be nice to let them down. Thankfully, he accepted this and gave her a lingering kiss.

Uneasy with seeing them kiss so passionately, Mary called over to her friend.

"Are you coming Pauline, it's time we were leaving." And she was relieved when they said their goodnights.

Don began to whistle as he strolled back to his billet. He was feeling very happy, and was wondering how a young English girl could have effected him so much. She was pretty, he knew that much, but he'd been with other pretty girls before and they had never left him feeling this way. A thought suddenly struck him. What if she didn't turn up for their date? Perhaps she had no intention of doing so. How would he feel then? He knew how he would feel. He would be devastated.

Having similar thoughts, Pauline had become very quiet on the walk home, and several times Kathy asked her if she was all right, with only a nod from Pauline in answer, until Clara could stand it no more and said loudly.

"Thinking about him I expect."

"Yeah! As a matter of fact Clara I was. Anything wrong in that?"

"Ask your Mam that question, why don't you? She will tell you what's wrong in that my girl."

"Come on girls, don't let's argue. Mary told them. "It was just a few dances. Where's the harm in that?"

"Nothing if that's all there is to it, but I reckon there's more to it than that."

"And if there is, what business is it of yours? Who made you my Mam any way? Just mind yer own bloody business will yer?" Pauline was already worried what her mam would do if she ever found out what she was up to, but she didn't need anyone reminding her of this.

"Pardon me for breathing. I was only looking out for you, that's all."

"Well don't. I'm a big girl now, an' I know how to look after meself."

"Charmed I'm sure."

Mary had had enough. "Stop it both of you. You sound like a couple of silly school kids. It's Pauline's life and if she wants to go out with a black man, well, that's up to her."

"I'll keep my mouth shut in future."

"Good," Pauline replied nastily.

The rest of the walk home was done in complete silence, until eventually, Clara made her apologies and there was peace at last.

"Hello Pauline love. Did you have a good night?"

"Yes, great Mam, thanks, but yer shouldn't have waited up for me."

"Oh I wouldn't sleep our Pauline, knowing that you weren't in."

"I saw Mary at the dance."

"Did you love, how is she?"

"Ok Mam. Would yer like me to make yer a cup of cocoa?"

"Yes please love, it might help me to sleep. I never got a wink last night, though I don't know why. I think I was worrying about our Ronald."

"Ahh! Was you?" Pauline didn't see the point of telling her Mam that she'd heard her snoring loudly during the night, and she let it pass. Edna was a delicate woman who did nothing but worry. Mostly about what the neighbour's might think of them but Pauline reckoned that if her Mam had nothing to worry about, she would worry. She smiled to herself at the thought of that, and was still smiling when she took Edna her cocoa.

"There you are Mam, that should help yer tonight."

"Thank you Pauline. You're a good girl, never an ounce of trouble. Not like some of the girls I've seen around. I don't know what some of the mother's are thinking of, letting their young"ens walk out with all sorts of different blokes. I'm glad you're not like that, I'd be six feet under with the worry."

Pauline almost choked on her drink, and felt the colour rise in her cheeks.

"Drink yer cocoa whilst it's warm Mam," she said, trying to change the subject, and then felt that she aught to mention the cinema.

"Would yer mind if I went to the pictures tomorrer Mam? Only one of the girls at work asked me and I said I'd ask yer."

"Mind? Of course I don't mind. Who is it? Do I know her?"

"No, she's not been there long. She's a nice girl though, so yer don't have to worry." She hated telling lies, but she couldn't tell her Mam that she was meeting a black man.

"I'm sure she is, I know you wouldn't go with anyone I wouldn't like. Will you be coming home first for your tea?"

"Yeah, 'cuz I'll have to get ready. I thought I'd go and have a look round town in me dinner break, and see if I can find a nice skirt to wear."

"Will you have enough coupons love?

"Just about I should think."

Edna's eyes were beginning to close and when she almost dropped her cup, she said. "I think I'll go to bed now Pauline. I'm that whacked out. Goodnight love, don't be too late coming up will you?"

"No Mam, I'm just finishing me cocoa then I'll follow yer."

It, actually, was quite a while after Edna had gone, that Pauline went to bed, because she'd laid back in her chair, her mind going over the nights events, especially the thoughts of Don, and how she couldn't wait to see him again.

2

Rushing home from work, Pauline put the bag that she was carrying, down onto the table. She had managed to buy a lovely grey skirt, but her day hadn't gone too well, with her mind being ruled by thoughts of Don and if he would be waiting for her. She had made several mistakes with her work, and as this was so unusual for her, her boss had been a little concerned and had asked if she was ill.

Seeing the bag with C&A written on the front of it, Edna was inquisitive as to what Pauline had bought.

"Come on, show me what you have will you?"

"Yes Mam, just let me get me coat off." And when she showed off the skirt, her Mam thought it beautiful.

"I like that. Did you have enough coupons love?"

"Yeah! Just."

Pauline put it on and waltzed around the living room, to show her mam. It clung to her hips, but fell into pleats from there to the hem. It was made in a woollen fabric, and on close inspection, you could just make out a dark blue check in it.

"What are you wearing with it?" Edna asked her.

"I thought me royal blue twin set. What do yer think?"

"Oh yes, that will go with it a real treat. Now then, take it off and come and eat these chips I've cooked for you. You don't want to be late for your friend." And Edna went into the kitchen to pour them both a cup of tea.

Sitting at the table, Pauline felt far too excited to eat, and when her mam asked her if she wasn't very hungry, she shook her head and pushed away the plate.

"Give them to me, I'll eat them, it's a shame to waste them," Edna said, reaching over to pick up the plate. She hadn't

18

bothered to cook herself anything, but seeing Pauline with her chips had made her feel hungry.

It took Pauline a good hour before she was ready to go out, but she thought it had all been worth it when she saw her reflection in the mirror. Her blonde hair was rolled back at the front of her head, but she had left the back hanging to her shoulders in a cascade of waves and curls, and when Edna saw her, she felt quite chuffed at having such a beautiful daughter.

"My! Pauline, you look really nice, and I do like your hair like that."

"Ahh! Thanks Mam."

"You"ll be having the boys after you tonight, looking like that."

"Don't be daft Mam." Pauline replied laughing, yet blushing for being so deceitful, and she was pleased to get outside where she didn't have to lie any more.

It was just on seven thirty when she arrived at the Odeon and Don was all ready waiting for her. Walking towards her, she could see by his face that he was pleased to see her, and taking her hand, he kissed her on her cheek.

"You look good enough to eat." He said smiling. "I could sit and look at you all night long."

"Wouldn't that be a waste of yer picture money?"

Who cares about money when I have you?"

Pauline giggled. "Get away with yer, yer silly fool. Yer making me blush."

Handing her a box of chocolates, Don told her that he'd already bought the tickets so that they didn't have to queue.

"Oh, so yer knew I'd be coming then?"

"Of course I did."

"Hark at you. Have they had the builders here today?"

Looking puzzled, Don asked her what she had meant.

"Well, they'd have to have 'em before you came tonight, or you'd never "ave got yer head through the door."

Don roared with laughter. "I fell for that one didn't I?"

"You certainly did, and I hope it teaches yer not to be so cocky in future." And she began to laugh too.

Don had booked one of the double seats in the balcony, and at first, he sat with one arm around her, but it wasn't long before they were kissing, and Pauline's heart was turning summersaults. Never before had she felt so much emotion, and if anyone had told her that she could feel this way, she would never have believed them.

It wasn't just Pauline who was having these feelings, for Don was too. He knew that Pauline was the girl that he'd been searching for, and how lucky he was to have found her. If nothing else, the war had found him someone special, and she felt very right for him. He'd had girl friends before, but none that made him feel this way, and if he hadn't come to England they might never have come to meet.

Putting her into a taxi for home, he was already looking forward to seeing her again. She had promised to meet him under Kemps Clock the following evening.

"Come on Mary, shift yourself or you"ll make us all late," shouted Clara, poking her friend in the ribs to wake her. "What's the matter with you? Are you ill? You're usually the first to get up."

"Leave me alone Clara will you. I'm not going in tonight. I can't face it."

"What do you mean you can't face it? Are you really ill? If you are I'll ask Mrs. Gray to keep an eye on you shall I? Is it your stomach?"

"I'm not ill, I just don't fancy going in, that's all. I didn't sleep too well and I'm tired."

"Oh we're all bloody tired, but someone has to make an effort to go in, or we might just as well surrender to the ruddy Germans. Come on now, Kathy's waiting down stairs."

"All right, I get the message. Keep your ruddy hair on will you?" And then after having a guilt trip, she said more kindly. "Give me five minutes and I'll join you."

"Good girl, I'll wait down stairs with Kathy." And as soon as Clara had left the room, Mary dragged herself from her bed, and began to get dressed. With only a quick splash to the face with cold water from the jug, she ran to catch up with her mates.

They were all on the night shift, so that meant trying to sleep during the day. Normally, Mary was a good sleeper, but today, she couldn't get her mind to relax at all. No matter how hard she tried to switch it off her thoughts were there to haunt her. What if Ron didn't come home? What if Ron got shot? How would she live knowing that he had never put his arms around her? She'd had a crush on him ever since he had offered to carry her case when she had first come to stay at Mrs. Gray"s.

"Can I help you with your case?" He'd called out to her when he'd seen her struggling.

"It's OK thanks, I'm sure I'll manage."

"I dare say you will, but why manage, when I could carry it for you?"

"I suppose you've got a point there," she'd replied laughing. "Thanks for the offer, it is a bit heavy."

Picking it up, Ron pretended to fall sideways. "Blimey! What you got in here? The kitchen sink? You girls always have to carry far too much stuff around."

"You offered to carry it, I didn't force it onto you."

Ron burst out laughing. "I was only joking. Actually it's quite light compared to what our Pauline drags around with her."

"Who's Pauline?"

"My sister. I'll introduce her to you one day. You'll like her. Most people do. We are very close considering we are only brother and sister. I expect it's because I looked out for her a lot when our Dad left us."

There was non stop chatter until Mary reached her lodgings, and reluctantly, she bid him goodbye, and thanked him for helping her.

The three girls only just managed to jump onto the tram before it left for town.

"Phew! That was a close call," Kathy said, sitting on one of the long wooden seats.

"Sorry you two. I should have got up earlier."

"Oh well, no harm done this time, but if it happens again, we'll leave without you. Ok?"

"It won't Kathy I promise you." And they arrived at work with only minutes to spare.

3

When Mary saw Pauline again she asked her if she thought Ron would like her to write to him.

"You know, just to cheer him up a bit I've heard that they look forward to news from home." She tried not to let Pauline see how keen she was, after all, she didn't want them to laugh at her behind her back. She had already asked if Ron had a girl friend, and when Pauline had said no, she didn't think there would be much of a chance of him asking her out, but to receive a letter from him would be very nice.

"I reckon he'd like that Mary. Naturally he gets them from me and me Mam, but I'm sure he'd appreciate hearing from you. I'll go and get yer his address." And true to her word Pauline returned with it.

With many screwed up balls of paper scattered across the table top, Mary thought she'd never find the right words to say, until at last, she decided to keep it as simple as possible.

Dear Ron,
I hope you don't mind me writing to you, but I thought it might help to keep you cheerful.
If you'd rather I didn't, just say the word and I won't send any more.
There have been a few raids during the past two weeks, but thankfully, none close to us. It's a nuisance getting out of a cosy bed to get to a shelter, but we mustn"t complain about that. I bet there are times when you wish you could get into a bed!
We went to the Astoria last week, and had a great time until Kathy got told to get off of the dance floor because she

was jitterbugging. She was still sulking about it the next day at work. We just couldn't shut her up and so one of the girls went and tied her scarf around her face so that she couldn't speak. You couldn't help but laugh, she looked so funny, as though she had a tooth ache. Luckily, she soon saw the funny side as well, and she didn't complain again.

I hope you are being fed well. Have you had any snails yet? I could never eat those things. Give me fish and chips any day. If you get a chance to write, I'd love to hear from you.
Take care, and give those Jerries a kick in the backside for starting the war. Bye for now.
-Mary

After putting it into an envelope and stamping it, she walked to the Loughborough Road where there was a red post box on one of the walls, but before she pushed her letter into it, she checked that no one was looking, before kissing her letter. "This one is for you, Ron," she whispered.

Returning to her lodgings, she found Pauline waiting for her.

"Hello Pauline, did you want me?"

"I was just wondering if yer had written your letter to our Ron yet?"

"I have just been to post one to him. Was there something that you wanted me to tell him for you?"

"Err, not exactly, it was more of something that I don't want yer to tell him."

"About Don you mean? Look Pauline, it's none of my business, so it's not for me to spread gossip about you. In any case, I wouldn't want him to have worries from home whilst he's fighting out there. It could be dangerous for him if he hadn't got his attention on the job he's doing."

"Thanks Mary, I really appreciate that. He might have written and mentioned it to my Mam, and she's enough on her plate already."

Like I said, it's none of my business, but if you're worried about your Mam, then perhaps you should think twice about seeing this Don feller?"

"I couldn't give him up Mary, 'cuz he's the best thing that's ever happened for me. Why should I have to give him up any way, just because his skin is a different colour to ours? He can't help what he was born with can he?"

"I know that sunshine, and I agree with everything you're saying, but I can still see it ending in tears, and I'd hate to see you get hurt. You're a good friend, and I'll always be here for you, no matter what, but like I said, I can't see a rosy future for you."

"It will be alright Mary, I know it will, I just need a bit more time before I tell me Mam about him. I'd die if I couldn't see him, 'onest I would."

"I can understand that love, I reckon we'd all do that, it's such a shame that your Mam doesn't think the same way that you do." Seeing Pauline looking so miserable, Mary added. "Take no notice of me love. Who am I to say what will or won't happen for you, and with this bloody war on, who the hell will care?" Then, as she walked towards her door, she stopped, turned around, and said. "Don't forget what I said about needing a friend. I'll always be here for you, so don't be afraid to come to me. OK?"

"Thanks Mary, I'll remember that. Ta ra."

"Ta ra Pauline."

Sitting in her room now, Mary could understand how Pauline felt. If Ron was her boyfriend she knew that she would be feeling the same way about him. How she longed to hear from him. Would he reply to her letter? She crossed her fingers for luck. Perhaps he and his mates would roll her letter up into a ball to use as a football. The wait to see if he would write was unbearable.

It was another two weeks before Mrs. Gray came knocking at her door.

"You in Mary?"

"Yes, come on in."

"I've brought this up for you, I thought it might be important to you," Mrs Gray told her as she handed her an air mail letter. "Have you a friend in the forces?"

"It"ll be from Pauline's brother Ron. I said I'd write to him, so as he'd get more letters like." Mary was trying her hardest not to give anything away, but when Mrs. Gray ranted on about the war and the rationing, she wanted to shout, go away and let me read my letter, but instead, she pretended to be interested in all that her landlady was going on about. It was such a relief when she told Mary that she had to go and get on with the potatoes she was in the middle of peeling.

Excited now, Mary tore open her letter.

Dear Mary,

What a pleasure it was to receive your letter, and such a nice surprise. Thank you for thinking of me. It really cheered me up, especially the bit about Kathy. I can just see her face now. You tell her from me, that the Astoria doesn't know what it's missing until they've seen Kathy jitterbug. She does it brilliantly. I only wish I was there to go with you all. I do miss it, and all of you. Never mind, as soon as we get this war over with we'll be able to go where we like. We just have to get rid of Hitler first. We can't let him win. Can you imagine what life would be like for us all if he got himself in charge of everyone. It doesn't bear thinking about does it?

Two of our young lads were shot last night, and neither of them survived. Poor sods. Forgive me for swearing Mary, but that's how this war gets to you.

Anyway, enough of the war. You won't want to write to me again if I only send you miserable letters.

How are Mam and Pauline? I expect Mam is worrying her socks off, and Pauline is out every night enjoying herself. Not that I blame her of course. You tell her to keep well away from those American G.I.'s. I've heard that they have arrived in Leicester.

Please write again, and send any news you have. Take care.

-Ron

Mary read and reread it several times before placing it under her pillow, and then, after shampooing her hair, and setting it with dinky curlers, she sat at the table to write a reply.

Hello Ron,

Thanks for your letter. It was great to receive it, although I felt quite sad about the boys that were killed. How unfair to lose their lives like that. Their poor Mum's must be broken hearted. There is nothing gained from wars is there? Only loss of life and sadness. Please keep yourself safe won't you?

Your Mam and Pauline are both fine so don't worry about them.

We are having to work very hard to keep everything up to date for you soldiers, after all, I'd hate it to be on my conscience that someone had died because I wasn't doing my job properly. It's nice to know that women can do their bit too.

We have had a lot of evacuee's arriving in Leicester, mostly from around the London area. Can you imagine how their Mothers feel, having to hand their children over to someone that they don't know, but at least, they will stand more chance of survival here.

One of the girls at work is thinking of joining the land army. I wouldn't mind that myself. What do you think? Would you like me in that uniform? I'm looking forward to seeing you in yours. I bet you look dead handsome, and all the girls will flock around you. That's if I don't trip them up first of course.

I've enclosed a photo of myself. I had it taken at Jerome's. You can stick it up somewhere so's you and your mates can throw darts at it if you like.

Cheers for now.

-Mary

Ron's reply came back much quicker than she had expected, and she ripped it open with excitement.

My dear Mary,

I do so look forward to your letters reaching me. They give me something to live for, and when I feel down I read them to brighten me up again. Thanks for the photo. I showed it to the lads and they were quite envious. You look stunning on it. I'll certainly not throw darts at it, and Lord help anyone else if they do it. I have put it in my wallet to keep it safe.

I was wondering if, when I'm next on leave, you would come out on a date with me. I've been wanting to ask you for ages, but you know what we men are like. Afraid of getting a rejection. If you answer by letter and say no, well, you won't see the disappointment on my face will you? Let me know what you decide.

Please don't join the land army, I've heard what some of those farms hands are like, and it would only make me jealous. Please write again soon.

-Ron. xx

Mary thrilled both by the invite and also for the two kisses he had added at the end of the letter, could hardly stop herself from broadcasting her news, but she didn't want to tell anyone yet, because it was too soon. Anything could happen, and she'd look silly if nothing came of it. She was already wishing that his next leave would come quickly, and she didn't need any persuading to sit and write her answer. If only he'd known how much she had been praying for him to ask her out, he would be very surprised.

4

"Are you out again tonight our Pauline? You never seem to be in these days. I get so fed up sitting on my own every evening. Can't you stay in tonight and keep me company?"

"I can't tonight Mam, 'cuz I've promised me mate I'd meet her, and if I don't turn up, she'll have hung around for nothing, and she might not bother with me again. I'll stay with yer tomorrer, will that be all right?"

"I expect it"ll have to be. Who is this girl any way? Do I know her? You seem to spend a lot of time with her. You don't usually bother so much. Why don't you invite her home so as I can meet her. You're not ashamed of me are you?"

"Of course I'm not Mam. Don't talk like that. I don't like it. Yer know I love yer to bits. Yer the best Mam anyone could have. Look, I will bring her home sometime, but she works funny hours, so I usually meet her straight from work."

"I don't know where you find to go all the time, or how you can afford it."

"Just here an' there Mam, just here an' there. We don't spend much because we often go for a walk or go to the Abbey Park. It gives us a bit of fresh air after sitting in a factory all day."

"Well, I can understand that, but Maud next door says that she's seen young girls walking out with those Americans that are around. I don't want you going with them. Do you hear?"

"I hear yer Mam. I'm off now. Don't wait up for me will yer? Ta ra." And she was glad to get outside before her Mam could see the guilt written all over her face. She'd hated telling lies, but she knew that her Mam would have forbid her to go out if she had known the truth. Don being black and American was double trouble if her Mam ever found out about him. I'm going to have to be careful that nosey old Maud doesn't see us. She thought.

Pauline and Don met underneath Kemps clock as arranged. It was the normal place for people in Leicester to meet up. As usual, Don was there first, and a broad beam crossed his face when he set eyes on her.

"Where shall we go tonight then?" he asked her.

"I don't mind. Where would yer like to go?"

"Some of my friends are meeting at a club on the Saffron Lane. Would you like to go there? They have dancing tonight."

"Yeah! Sounds good to me." And arm in arm they walked towards that way. It took them longer than they had thought, because they kept stopping for a kiss and a cuddle, but it was a nice evening, so they found the walk relaxing.

They were almost at the club when Don stopped in his tracks, making Pauline stumble.

"What did yer do that for?" she yelled at him.

"Shhh, get down." And Don shoved her down under a tree to hide her. It was at this point that Pauline also heard the plane flying above them, and she could tell by the look on Don's face that it wasn't one of theirs. At first they thought it was going away, but it turned again, and Don, so afraid that they would be seen, lay himself on top of Pauline to protect her. The plane passed over them and moved on further before dropping its bombs. It wasn't until they were sure it had flown away into the distance, that they both sat up.

"Are you alright Pauline?" Don asked.

"Yes thanks. I'm fine. How about you?"

"I'm alright. I'm sorry if I hurt you when I pushed you down. I was afraid for you."

"I can smell fire. I wonder where he dropped them. They stood up to have a look around. It looks as though it is in Cavendish Road. I wonder if anyone is hurt."

"Mm, I was thinking the same thing. Do you think we should take a look to see if there is anything we can do? Can we get through from here?"

"Yes it's just down here. Come on I'll show yer."

Reaching the scene, they found people crying, and neighbours were checking to see who needed their help. Don helped to move a load of bricks that were blocking the way of the ambulances and the fire brigade, whilst Pauline went to help a lady holding a baby, too distressed to know what she was doing. Everyone was helping out. It was like a team relay race, as they passed water in buckets to try and put out smaller fires.

Exhausted and dirty, Pauline and Don left as soon as they knew that there was nothing more that they could do, but there spirits were low, as they realised how close they had been to death. Don pulled Pauline close to him, as though he would never let her go again, and Pauline cried on his shoulder.

"I don't know what I would have done if anything had happened to you Pauline."

They sat to rest on some grass, hidden by trees from the road, and they sat huddled together for several minutes, until Pauline looked up at him and said:

"Don make love to me."

"No Pauline we mustn't, it wouldn't be right. We'll regret it tomorrow."

"I thought you loved me."

"You know I do, and that is why we can't."

"Prove it to me then."

"Pauline, stop it. You're not being fair."

"Fair? Who cares about fair when planes come and drop their bombs on people, not caring if they get hurt. What's fair about that Don? Tell me that?" Pulling his face to hers she began to kiss him until he could resist her no more, and they made unbelievable love until they were both spent, and then afterwards, they lay in each other's arms as though united, until Don whispered:

"I'm sorry Pauline. I didn't mean to let it happen."

Pauline looking into his face told him, "No, don't be sorry. It's what I wanted. I'm glad we did it. It was beautiful for me Don. I'll never regret it. I love you so much."

"And I love you too. One day when this war is over, will you marry me?"

"Of course I will. I'll never forget this day as long as I live."

Edna sat knitting, and Pauline, irritated by the clicking of the knitting needles, turned up the radio to drown out the noise. Now that Don had made love to her, she felt that it was time to tell her Mam about him, but where did she start. She couldn't just blurt out. Mam I'm going out with a black American, and last night we had sex. No! That would kill her. Every now and again, she plucked up courage to tell her, but the courage didn't last long enough for her to come out with it. Then she had an idea to try out the water.

"Mam…."

"Mmm?." Edna said, still concentrating on her knitting.

"There's a girl at work who's going out with an American soldier."

Edna tutted with disgust. "I wonder what her mother thinks of that."

"She hasn't told her yet."

"Then it's time that she did, and I hope her mother puts a stop to it when she does."

"He's black."

Edna almost dropped her knitting in surprise. "Good lord, it gets worse. If you know her Mother our Pauline, I hope you will let her know what's going on behind her back."

"Why? She said they love each other. What's wrong in that?"

"What's wrong with it? I'll tell you what's wrong with it my girl. The man comes from a different country, and being black, he comes from a different culture. It could never work."

"It could if they really wanted it to."

"I've told you before Pauline, mixed marriages never work. Now let's talk about something else. You know how I feel about these things so there's no point in discussing it any more, so shut up and let's listen to Itma."

Pauline could see the temper rising up in her Mam, and she didn't know how she was going to break her news to her. She felt it best to leave it for another day, and offered to make supper, and it wasn't long before they were both laughing at Itma on the radio.

5

Kathy, Mary, and Clara were getting ready to go to the dance at the Palais, and that afternoon, they had been to town to buy new clothes to wear. It was a new month of their ration books, so they had gone a little mad and used quite a few. Kathy had bought a new green dress with a sweetheart neck line, and Mary and Clara had both bought a new skirt each. They had also treated themselves to new underwear, and Kathy had bought herself a bra, with cups that went into a point. Mary had never seen anything so funny, and was in hysterics.

"I don't know why you find it so funny Mary," Kathy said crossly. "We weren't all born so well endowed as you. Some of us are grateful for a little extra help."

"Put it on Kathy," Clara begged. "Let's see how it looks on you." But when Kathy did put it on, she too burst out laughing, making Kathy even angrier.

"Just stop it will you. I wish I'd never shown it to you now." This made the other two girls laugh more, and all they could do was to fall in the floor in hysterics.

"Stop it Mary," Clara begged. "I've got the bloody stitch from laughing so much, but instead of helping, Mary laughed even louder, until in the end, Kathy, unable to stop herself, began to laugh with them until all three were exhausted.

Wiping her eyes, Mary said, "That's the best ruddy laugh all week, and it took a bra to do it." And set them all off laughing again.

"Do your boobs go to the end of the point Kathy?" Clara asked.

"Of cause they don't you daft devil. Who the hell has a bust that goes to a point? I bet you don't know anyone."

"I do," Mary told them.

"Who?"

"You!" And again they burst into fits of laughter.

"What are you going to fill the ends with?" Clara asked between giggles.

"Nothing. You don't need to. Look. They're quite hard." But when Kathy pushed one of the points to show them, the end piece suddenly went in, leaving her with one pointed boob and one flat ended one, which set them all off again.

"I've got some cotton wool in my room," Mary told her. I'll go and get it and you can stuff the end with that, otherwise when you dance with a bloke, he might lean towards you, and you'll have two flat ends. There, that's better," she added when Kathy had stuffed the cotton wool inside. "You can't tell they are not all yours now."

When they were dressed and ready to go, they shouted to Mrs. Gray that they wouldn't be too late getting in.

"I hope Graham is there this week," Clara told the others. He wasn't there the last time we went. If he was on a date with that Betty Andrews, I won't speak to him again. She's been after him for ages, always making eyes at him and fluttering her eyelashes, and that bright red lipstick she wears makes her look a right trollop."

"Hasn't he asked you out yet Clara?"

"No Mary. I sometimes wonder if he ever will, but I still keep hoping. He's always wanting to dance with me, but that's all."

"I don't know why you bother. You wouldn't find me waiting for some bloke to ask me out," Kathy chimed in.

"I know you're right Kathy, but I can't help who I fancy can I?"

"I suppose not. Have you thought of making him jealous? If you did, at least you'd know if he really was interested in you or not. Flirt with someone else and try to ignore Graham. See what his reaction to that is."

"It's worth a try I suppose. Ok! I'll do it, but it won't be easy to ignore him, especially if that Betty is hanging around him."

As usual the dance hall was packed out, but Clara was still able to pick Graham out from all the rest. He was with his mates and they stood at the side of the room chatting. Seeing Clara come in, he stopped and looked at her smiling, but Clara pretended that she hadn't seen him, and walked straight past him, and it wasn't long before someone came to ask her to dance.

"What's your name?" the boy was asking her now.

Not really interested, Clara told him hers, but didn't bother to ask him his until they were dancing in front of Graham, and then she asked flirtingly, "What's your name?"

Thinking that she fancied him, the lad pulled her closer to him, and put his cheek next to hers. Clara didn't like that, especially when she could smell his B.O. but she had to put up with it for now. Suddenly, the bloke was pushed aside, and Graham was standing between them.

"I don't like other blokes dancing with my girl," he told the lad, and grabbing Clara around the waist he began to dance with her.

"Who are you to tell me who I can dance with? I'm not your girl, so why did you say that?"

"You are now."

"Oh am I? I don't remember you asking me."

"Clara Martin, will you be my girl?"

"Of cause I will. I thought you'd never ask, but you go any where near that Betty Andrews, and it'll be all over. Do you understand?"

Graham laughed loudly.

"So, what's so funny?"

"You are. I can't stand the girl. She gets on me nerves, keep following me everywhere. I won't two-time you I promise." And he pulled her to him and kissed her, making Clara melt inside.

6

Pauline had already missed one period, and with the day's passing and no sign of a second one, she was pretty sure that she must be pregnant. She couldn't go to the doctor until she was at least three months, because they couldn't tell before that. She knew it was her own fault, but that didn't stop the panics of what her Mam would do to her when she found out, and what would Don think about it? Would he be angry with her? Her head was spinning around in all directions. What the hell was she going to do? She needed someone to talk to. She couldn't cope with this alone, but who? And then she remembered what Mary had told her about being there for her.

Tapping on Mary's door now, she was relieved to find Mary alone.

"Hello sunshine. Anything I can do for you?"

"Err; no Mary, I just thought I'd pop in an' see yer. Were yer busy?"

"I'm doing nothing that can't wait. Come on in. I was only going to set my hair with some sugar and water."

"Me Mam does that, and then she wonders why all the wasps keep following her around."

"I know what you mean. Flies too for that matter. The things we do for beauty eh?"

Mary noticed that Pauline seemed a little nervous, and guessed that this was more than a social visit, but she decided that when Pauline was ready, she'd tell her the real reason for her visit.

"Cup of tea Pauline?"

"Yes please Mary, I wouldn't mind."

When they sat on the edge of Mary's bed to drink it, Pauline suddenly blurted out.

"Mary? Is it possible to be pregnant after only one time of doin' it?"

Alarm bells rang in Mary's head and she tried to answer her friend calmly but truthfully.

"I expect so love. Those bloody sperms seem to be able to swim anywhere. They don't care whether it's your first time or your hundredth. Dead inconsiderate they are sometimes. Why do you ask? Do you know someone it's happened to?"

"Well, yeah, I do. There's this girl at work, and she's worried what her family will think of her. She was asking if I knew anyone she could go to for help like?"

"She doesn't want to mess with those people love. Girls have been made very ill because the woman didn't know what she was doing properly. It's not worth the risk. Does she really want to be rid of it?"

"No, 'cause she don't. She loves the bloke, and she knows he'll marry her, but her Mam'll kill her when she finds out."

"Pauline look at me. It's you isn't it?"

Pauline nodded and then burst into tears. "What am I going to do Mary?"

"Have you told Don yet?"

"No. I was hoping it was a false alarm, and I'd be alright, but this is the second month I've missed."

Mary put her arms around her. "Worrying isn't going to help love. What's done is done. You're going to have to break the news to him and your Mam soon." There was Ron too. He'd already been worried about Pauline going out with one of the Yanks, but when he finds out that this one is black too, she daren't imagine what he'd do. Would he be cross with her for not telling him. If only Pauline had heeded what she'd been telling her for ages, that Don was big trouble. "What do you think Don will say when you tell him Pauline."

"I know he'll want to marry me Mary."

"Well, at least you"ll be able to depend on him. The biggest problem will be your Mam. When are you going to tell her?"

"I daren't even think about it. Would you be with me when I tell 'er?"

"Oh I don't know about that. I don't really want to get too involved. I have to think of me and Ron as well." But when Pauline burst into tears again, she relented and said. "Alright Pauline. I will if that's what you want."

"Thanks Mary yer a real mate."

Mary didn't like the idea of letting Edna know that she had known about Pauline and Don, but the girl needed a friend right now, and she had promised to be there for her, so she couldn't go back on her word, even though she thought Pauline should have had more sense than to go and get herself pregnant.

Returning home exhausted, Pauline went to bed early. Mainly because she couldn't face her Mam any more that night, and she didn't want her to see that she had been crying in case she began to ask questions. She was glad that she'd had a chat to Mary, because it had eased her a little, and tomorrow, she would tell Don.

Hardly able to put one foot in front of the other through lack of sleep, Pauline made her way to meet Don. She hoped that his reaction to becoming a father, wouldn't be a horrible one. Perhaps he would tell her it served her right for tempting him to make love to her. She felt so nervous and wished that Mary were with her. She'd always relied on other people, but now she was alone, and she was hating having to tell him.

"Hello darling." he said putting his arm around her. "Had a good day?"

"Mmm, what about you?"

"Not much different to any other day. The sergeant has been bellowing again, and made us re- clean our shoes, because one of the lads hadn't bothered to clean his. He said we were a rotten shower, and to get some spit and polish on them."

"I'd have told him where to get off if he'd shouted at me."

"Oh we do that alright. But not to his face of course."

"Don...?"

"Yes love?"

"I've got something I need to tell yer."

"Fire away. I'm listening." But as she was about to break her news to him, one of his mates came up and slapped him on his back.

"Do you think we have a chance of beating them tonight Don?" he asked, before saying hello to Pauline.

"We'd better Greg. We haven't played this team before have we?"

"No but I'm looking forward to it. Are you two coming to watch?"

"I wouldn't mind. What about you Pauline? Are you up to watching a game of baseball. It'll be on the Abbey Park."

"I don't mind if that's what you'd like Don."

"Great. I think you"ll enjoy it. Oh sorry Pauline. You were about to tell me something. What was it?"

"It's nothing important Don. It can wait."

Greg saw a bus pulling into the park. "That looks like our rivals," he told Don.

"So it is. They look a burly lot don't they?"

"It's not size that matters man, it's how fast you can run."

"We should be ok, with Bill on our team. You can't get faster than him."

In the park, Don lay his coat down on to the grass for Pauline to sit on, and she knew that there would be no chance to have a serious talk to Don with Greg tagging along, and when their team had won, Don and Greg danced around as though they had just won a fortune. It was another hour before Greg decided to leave them alone. And Don was still going on about the baseball game.

"We won Pauline," he kept saying, and once, he even picked her up and swung her around to show how pleased he was, until in the end she had to beg him to stop. He was so happy, that she wondered how she could break her news to him.

"Don, I have to talk to yer."

"Ok love. I'm all yours now."

Shaking, she began.

"I've missed twice Don."

"Missed what twice love?"

"Yer know! That!"

Don scratched his head. What on earth was she talking about? And then it suddenly dawned on him.

"You mean?"

"That's right."

Don came down to earth with a bump.

"Oh my giddy aunt, Pauline. Are you sure you've got it right?"

"Of course I'm sure. What are we gonna do?"

"All we can do. Get married of course."

"Do yer mean that?"

"Of course I mean it. We'll just be married sooner than later that's all. Stop worrying, I'll have a son I can teach baseball to."

"Fine except for one thing. It might be a girl."

"Well if she's half as pretty as you, I won't mind a bit."

"I don't know what me Mam will say, when she finds out Don."

"I'll have to meet her now Pauline. We can't put it off any longer. I'll see my C.O. tonight when I get back and explain the situation to him, and see if he can arrange for us to be married quickly."

"Yer a good bloke Don and I don't deserve yer."

"Don't talk like that. I'm no better than you. We love each other Pauline and that's the most important thing."

"I don't know how I'm going to tell me Mam."

"We'll do it together. I'll have to meet her now. Let me see the C.O. first and then we can tell your mum about the wedding."

42

"Thanks Don for not letting me down."

"You know I wouldn't do that Pauline. I've told you. I love you. We're in this together."

Throwing his kit bag onto the rack of the train, Don was still very angry with his Commanding officer, and he sat down with a thump. Did that man have any feelings at all? How could he do this to him, and what would Pauline think? He had given his word to her, that everything would be all right, and now, he couldn't even get a message to her.

He'd told his C.O. everything and had said how much he had wanted to marry Pauline, but instead of congratulations, he was told that that would be impossible, as he was being shipped abroad immediately. Don had protested, and asked if he could have the wedding first, but the officer had stuck to his word and refused him.

"You will be on the next plane out, so get your things ready at once." he had been told.

"Sir, I can't do that. I've promised my girl."

"You will do as ordered man, and I'll have no more of your back chat. Now get going."

And Don was taken to the station by armoured guard to make sure that he was on the train to the airport.

7

Ron had written to tell Mary that he had a weekends leave coming up the following weekend, and if she liked, she could meet him off of the train.

Both nervous and excited, Mary had dressed in her favourite wine coloured dress which looked good with her brown hair. She had slept all night with her curlers in, although sleeping, wasn't the right word to use, as they had painfully kept her awake for most of the night, as they stuck into her head and ears. She had tried sleeping face down, but found that to be uncomfortable. She hoped that her eyes didn't show the tiredness that she was feeling. She had tied her hair up on to the top of her head with a comb, giving her a lot of curls bunched together. Luckily, Don had given Pauline some nylons for them all, and with a pair of kid gloves on her hands to save laddering them, she put a pair on. Checking that the seams were straight, she then put on her grey duster coat, and a silk scarf to tie around her neck.

Standing on the station platform, she waited for the train to pull in. There seemed to be more soldier's heads hanging out of the window than in, and it was difficult to see who you were looking for with them all wearing the same uniform. Mary scanned them looking for Ron, and turned quickly when she heard him calling to her.

"Mary, hey Mary," he called waving to her, and she began to run alongside the train to keep up with him until it came to a stop.

Jumping down from his compartment, he took her into his arms, and said: "God! You look good Mary. I've been dreaming of this day ever since you agreed to go out with me. You haven't changed your mind now that you've seen me again have you?"

"Don't be daft. It's been a long wait for you to come home, and I'm looking forward to spending time with you."

"Good. That's a relief."

Putting his free arm around her, and throwing his kit bag onto his other shoulder, they began to walk towards the station steps, and as they reached them, people began patting him on his shoulder, saying, "Well done son. We're all grateful to you lads fighting for us. Then another shouted God bless, and may he keep you safe."

It was all a bit too much for Ron and he began to feel embarrassed.

"Wasn't that kind?" Mary told him. But all Ron could do was to squeeze her hand in answer. People like that, do make it all worth while, he thought.

Edna kept looking out of the window to see if they had arrived yet. Mary had told her that she was meeting Ron, and that they would come straight home, and Edna had laid the table out with a clean cloth and some sandwiches to welcome them.

It was twelve o'clock when she heard them coming down the entry, and she rushed to open the door ready for them. Ron, throwing his bag down gave her a hug, and asked her how she was.

"All the better for seeing you our Ron. I do miss you."

"Never mind, it won't be for much longer Mam, I reckon we'll all be on our way home soon."

"That's what everyone was saying last year, and you're still fighting. Come on in Mary and sit yourself down love. Thanks for meeting him."

"No trouble Edna, I enjoyed it, we've been having a laugh, and the folks on the station were really kind to him."

"Where's our Pauline?" Ron was asking now. "She's usually the first to meet me."

"She's up the yard. She's been there for ages. Will you give her a shout to let her know you are here?"

"It's ok, I'll go. You have a chat to your Mam," Mary told him, but secretly, she was wondering if Pauline was alright.

"You alright Pauline?" she shouted through the toilet door.

"Not really Mary. I can't stop being sick. I was about to come out when yer called." And when she emerged Mary became worried about how pale her mate looked.

"If it happens again, I'll have to tell Ron I've got some bug or something."

"Pinch your cheeks a bit, so you don't look so peaky. There, that's a bit better."

"Am I showing yet Mary? I don't want him to know."

"No, love you're fine, now come on, we'd better show our faces." But as they began to walk to the back door, Ron was coming out to hurry them up."

"There you are. I was beginning to think you'd fell down the hole, and I needed a rope to get you out."

"I see yer still as cheeky as ever, our Ron. I'd 'ave thought the army would have taught yer better."

"You should know better than that sis. It'd take more than the army to sort me out. What you see is what you get. Now, are you going to give your brother a big hug?" And Pauline ran into his open arms. He felt so comfortable, as though things didn't seem half as bad when he was around.

"You seem to be feeding yourself well our kid. I can feel your hips getting bigger. Have you been eating too many of those dried egg sandwiches Mam makes you?"

"It's only puppy fat our Ron," Edna said as they walked in through the kitchen door.

"I know Mam, I was only teasing her." Then he asked. Any tea in the pot Mam? No one makes a cuppa like you do."

"Yes. Sit yourselves down and I'll pour it out. Get tucked in to those sandwiches all of you, before they start curling up at the edges." And not another noise came from them until they were fed and nourished.

"Do you mind if Mary and I go for a walk Mam?"

"Mind? Of course not love. You go and enjoy yourselves." She was hoping that his friendship with Mary might develop into something better than just friends, and she was pleased when he'd included Mary in his walk. She liked Mary a lot, and felt that she would be good for her son.

Walking down the black pad towards the river, Mary and Ron held hands as they walked underneath the trees that were bowed over, making an archway to the little bridge that divided the brook from the river. The sunlight shone in and out between the branches of the trees making them feel relaxed. It was a place where the war was forgotten about for a while, as though they were taken away from the rest of the world, and transported into a place of haven. Mary had never felt so happy as now, and sometimes Ron would turn and smile at her, and squeeze her hand as though she were someone special to him. The months of waiting for this moment were long passed, and this was a dream come true. How she wished that he didn't have to leave her again. Life without him was no fun, and she would pray that his next leave would come very soon.

Leaning over the side of the bridge, Ron put his arm around her waist as they watched the water rippling over the pebbles, and the fish swimming in and out of them. The sun shone onto their faces making them feel happy and calm, and they stood there for a while, breathing in the freshness of the air around them, before continuing their journey towards Birstall. When they reached the field with it's mown hay, they sat down to rest, and lying down, Ron picked a long blade of grass and put it in his mouth to chew the end, but his eyes were focused onto Mary. The sunlight was throwing shades of brown and auburn from her hair. She turned to look at him, and he smiled, threw away the grass, and pulled her gently to the floor beside him, and then, resisting it no longer, he kissed her, tenderly at first, and then with passion as she responded to him. Between the kisses, he told her how much he'd longed for the day he could be with her like this, and had wondered if it would ever happen.

"It's a funny world," Mary told him. "I felt the same way about you too."

"Too afraid of being turned down I suppose."

"Silly isn't it?"

"Mmm! Very silly." And they both lay very still with their arms around each other.

"I love you Mary."

"Do you Ron?"

"Yes Mary, I do. Will you be my girl?"

"Try stopping me."

When they told Edna that they were officially courting, she was thrilled to bits. "I'm so happy. I'd hoped you would." And she hugged them both, whilst Pauline thought it great news.

8

As the months passed, Pauline was finding it more and more difficult to get into her clothes, and kept buying baggy tops to hide her stomach. How she missed Don. She didn't know why he hadn't met her that evening, and wondered if he was ill, but when she'd asked one of his friends, they had said they didn't think so, but they hadn't seen him for some time either. Pauline remembered the evening so well, she had stood under the clock for almost an hour in case he had been held up, but in the end, she had to admit that he wasn't coming, and had gone home to go to bed where she had cried. Even now, she knew that he must have a good reason, and that one day he would meet her again to explain. Mary had thought that he'd probably thought of himself being incapable of being a good father, and had returned home to get away from telling her, but Pauline wouldn't believe that. She knew Don too well, and knew that some day he would return to marry her.

Sitting with Mary now, they discussed the position that she was in, and Mary told her that now was the time to tell her Mam about the forth coming event.

"I daren't Mary. I don't know where to start."

"Well love, she's got to know sometime. There's no way you can hide a baby from her, and she's a right to know. Best do it sooner than later. Your Ron doesn't even know, and I feel guilty keeping it from him. Whenever he asks after you, I have to keep lying, and I don't like doing that to him. He'll think he can't trust me."

"I know yer right, an' I 'ave tried, honest I 'ave, but I get so nervous, I chicken out. If yer'd come with me, I'll tell her now." And fearing that Mary would say no, she began to beg. "Please Mary. It"ll be easier with you there."

49

"Alright, but I won't like it." And she put on a cardigan and followed Pauline to her house, but before going inside, Pauline asked her not to tell her Mam that Don was black.

"She's going to have to know sometime. It's not something she won't know for herself when she sees the child."

"I'll cross that bridge when I get to it. When it's born it'll be too late for her to do anything about it."

Feeling more nervous than she'd ever felt in her life, Pauline was pleased to see that her Mam was in a good mood.

"Hello Mary. It's nice to see you. Have you still got plenty of work?"

"Yes Edna, quite a lot."

"That's good. Sit down love. Sit down."

Pauline, looking towards Mary for encouragement, said, "Mam, I've got something to tell yer."

"Can it wait until Mary's gone home, only it seems a bit rude to talk when she's come to visit."

""No Mam. I asked Mary to come so's I can tell yer."

"Stop talking a load of nonsense Pauline, and spit it out. What do you mean you wanted Mary here? Then, panicking, Edna said, "It's not our Ron is it? Has something happened to him? Tell me Mary. Is he all right?"

"Yes Edna, as far as know, he's fine. I'm sorry if we upset you."

"Thank the Lord. You had me worried there. So, what is it you have to tell me? You're getting me into a right dither, with all this secrecy. Out with it Pauline will you?"

Pauline took a deep breath. "I'm pregnant Mam."

Edna almost fell out of her chair with shock. "Stop talking silly girl. You haven't even got a boyfriend as far as I know. When did it happen?"

" I do have a boyfriend, and we couldn't help it," Pauline began to cry.

"What the hell do you mean, you couldn't help it? Cause you could bloody help it, all you had to do was keep your legs closed. That's not too difficult is it?"

"Don't shout at me Mam. I've done it now, so it's too late."

"How far gone are you?"

"Five months."

"Five bloody months and you've only just told me?! I could knock your bloody head off for you. We'll be the laughing stock of the ruddy neighbourhood. Well, you can't keep it. You know that don't you."

"Why can't I? It's my baby, an' I won't give it away. Yer can't make me." And Pauline began to cry louder.

"Can't make you? I'll show you what I can do my girl. You can go and stay with your Auntie Molly, she's used to having girls like you in her house. She'll know what to do. Many a time she's looked after a pregnant girl before they hand the baby over for adoption. You can go on Wednesday. I'll write to her tonight to tell her to expect you. Where's the bloody father anyway? Turned on his heels has he, just like your Dad. Bloody typical. Leave it for the girl to sort it out eh?"

Mary was beginning to feel sorry for Pauline. Surely Edna could see how upset she was already, without getting on to her like that.

"I know you must be upset Edna, but perhaps when you've calmed down a bit, you'll think differently."

"Oh no I won't Mary. I've warned her many a time to be careful what she's doing, and she always looked at me so innocently. Well, I know now that she can't be trusted, and she's going to have to pay for it. How the hell would she be able to bring a baby up on her own? She'd have no future for a start off. Who'll want to marry her with a kiddie in tow. I've made my mind up and it's for her own good."

"My boyfriend will marry me Mam. He told me he would."

"So where is he then? Gone off with the bloody fairies? I thought you had more brains than that."

"He'll come back Mam, I know he will. He wouldn't let me down, he promised me, an' I believe him."

"Then you're dafter than I thought you were. I don't want to hear another word, you'll go to our molly's and no mistake." And when Pauline began to cry again, Edna told her, "It's no good crying. Go on get out of my sight, I can't bare to look at you any more tonight." Then turning to Mary she asked her not to write and tell Ron because she didn't want him getting upset. "We'll deal with this ourselves," she added.

Mary took Pauline back with her for a couple of hours. She knew that Edna was right about there being no future for Pauline with a baby, but if it had been her, she wouldn't have wanted to give it away either. How she wished Don had come when he had promised, but again she had to agree with Edna that it did seem as though he had done a runner. It's a good job Edna didn't know he was a black man, she'd have hit the roof and never come down again.

9

Molly was preparing the spare room for Pauline's stay. She had put clean bedding onto the bed, and had laid a clean blanket across the end of the bed in case Pauline felt cold in the night. The windows were polished until they shone, and although the blackout curtain wasn't very inviting, there was nothing she could do about that. At the side of the bed was a small table, and Molly had placed a cream crocheted cloth onto it, and had picked some yellow roses to go in a vase on top of it. Naturally, they would have to be taken out during the night time, but they could always be replaced in the mornings. Standing back to admire her effort, she felt that her niece would feel at home in the room. One thing that could be said about her sister, was that her house was always neat and tidy, and she didn't want her to think that she couldn't do as good.

She wondered why Edna wasn't coming with Molly, and had left it to Ron's girlfriend to bring her instead. Molly had a few girls to stay until they had their babies, and she had seen how upsetting it was for them to give their child up. After all, they had carried them for nine months, and at the end, they had nothing to show for it. What a shame that Pauline was to go through the same thing. Had Pauline been her daughter, she would have helped her to bring it up, but not Edna.. She'd be too bothered about what other people would think.

Often, she'd get a visit from one of the girl's she had helped, and Molly would listen as they spoke of their depressions from having to give their baby away. Life could be very unfair, especially for women.

Pauline would arrive at any minute, and Molly had already placed the kettle onto the fire to boil, and when there came o knock at the door, she opened it with excitement. It was good to see Pauline, it was just a shame that it had to be this way, but she'd look after her as best she possibly could.

"Hello Pauline, come on in love." And giving her a hug, she saw Mary standing back a little. "Come on in Mary love. It's nice to meet you at last. I've heard a lot about you. Did you have a good journey?"

"Not bad thanks Aunt Molly."

"We'll have a cup of tea first, and then I'll take you up to your room, so's you can put your things away. I bet you're ready for a cup of tea aren't you?"

"Yes please Molly," Mary replied. "It was quite warm on the train, and the smoke does sting your mouth a bit."

"Tell me about it. You can taste it for ages afterwards. There you are both of you, drink that up."

"Thank you Molly," Mary said, but Pauline hardly said a word as they sat together.

Molly nodded to Mary. "She'll be alright once she gets settled Mary. I find all the girls are like this when they first come."

Taking them up to the room, Molly stood aside to let the other two walk through the door first. Mary thought it a delightful room, and expressed her feelings to Pauline, but all Pauline could do was to nod in agreement.

After a couple of hours, Mary left them, but she didn't go with an easy mind. She felt very concerned for her friend, and wished that there was something she could do to make it right for her.

Molly and Pauline sat outside in the garden. Molly was sewing, and Pauline was laid back in her chair with her eyes closed. She was beginning to feel more relaxed. Opening her eyes for a second, she noticed the butterflies dancing in and out of the buddleia tree. She watched until her eyes, growing heavy, began to shut again, and it wasn't long after that she fell asleep. She was in great need of sleep, as she hadn't slept at all well, since her Mam had told her that she couldn't keep her baby. Most of her last two nights had been spent crying, both for her baby and for Don. How would he find her if she wasn't in Leicester? He had promised that everything would be alright, and it wasn't. Suddenly, she jumped and woke up.

"What's the matter love? Were you having a bad dream?"

"I'm not sure Aunt Molly, I thought I felt me belly jump. Yes, there it goes again. Feel it Aunt Molly. Quick put yer hand on it. Can yer feel it? It's my baby moving isn't it?"

"Yes, it seems like it doesn't it? Never having a child of my own, I couldn't swear to it, but I can't think of what else it could be."

Pauline stroked her stomach before whispering. "Hello baby, are you moving about in there? Yer Mammy loves yer an' she won't let anyone take yer away from me, I promise. Yer Daddy will come soon, an' we'll all live in a little house with a garden for yer to play in." She then burst into tears. "Aunt Molly, I can't give it away, I can't."

Molly wished that she had the right words to make her feel better, and seeing how upset her niece was, she had to wipe a tear from her own eyes. All that she could do, was to hold her close and cuddle her. "I'll go and make you a nice cup of tea shall I?"

Pauline nodded, and Molly went into the house, whilst Pauline lay back in her chair again, but sat up, when she heard the click of the garden gate. Walking in was a tall man with stubble on his chin, and greasy hair. He looked as though he hadn't bathed for months. Seeing Pauline, he grinned broadly, showing his dirty broken teeth.

"My! You're a pretty one. Where did Molly get you from eh? I suppose you're like all the others she has here. Got yourself up the duff have you?"

Pauline didn't like him at all. She thought him rude and rough.

"Yes I'm pregnant, though what it's got do with you?"

"Oh nothing," he replied laughing. "I swear I never came near you." And thinking that was funny, he laughed louder than ever.

"Believe me, whoever yer are, I wouldn't let yer. Look at the state of yer for one thing."

The man roared with laughter. "I like you. I wouldn't mind you for myself."

"In yer dreams."

"Oh hello Frank, I didn't hear you come. Have you met my niece Pauline?"

"Sort of Molly, sort of. I was about to introduce myself when you came out." Frank put on his posh speaking voice, as he always did for Molly. After all, she was his boss, and he enjoyed working in her garden.

"Frank is one of our neighbours Pauline. He works as a gardener for me, so you'll be seeing a lot of him."

Pauline hoped not, but didn't say as much.

"I'll fetch another cup Frank then you can have a cup of tea with us. I'll get that money I owe you for the rose bush too whilst I'm inside."

"Thank you Molly. That's very kind."

After Molly had gone back inside the house, Frank turned his attention back to Pauline. "So you're her niece are you? Then you'll get preferential treatment won't you? How lucky to have an Aunt who takes care of immoral girls like you."

"Don't yer dare call me immoral, I'm no such thing." Pauline was furious with him. "Yer don't know anything about me, so how dare yer call me that. Yer should take a look in yer mirror sometime, then yer might get a nasty shock yerself."

"Oh, feisty eh? I like a girl with spirit. Anytime you fancy a night out, just give old Frank a call."

"No thanks, yer the last person I'd go out with."

Frank threw back his head and laughed out loud. "The more I gets to know you, the more I gets to like you."

Molly, hearing him laugh, hoped that he had cheered Pauline up a little. What a good job he came to visit today. They might get on really well together. She thought. Frank had always seemed to be a well-mannered man, and always kind to her girls, although you got the odd one who didn't seem to take to him, but you can't win them all. She went and paid Frank the money that she owed him, and poured out his tea.

"Isn't this cozy?" she said out loud.

"Yes, very nice Molly. I must say, that lavender smells delightful. Don't you think so Pauline?"

Cringing, Pauline would have preferred not to answer, but did so for the sake of her Aunt, but all she could muster was a "yes." She didn't like him one iota, and wished that he would go home. How her Aunt got taken in by him was anyone's guess, but he knew how to play up to her, that's for sure.

Frank was talking now to Molly. "I have a lot of respect for you Molly. It can't be easy taking in girls like this. What made you do it?"

"Because I feel so sorry for them Frank. Turned out of their own homes, and having to give up their babies must be awful for them. It takes two to tango, yet the man can walk away from it all, without a slur on his character. There are times when I wish I could keep both girl and her baby, but that would be impractical for me. You can't keep them all can you? Naturally, I never thought that I'd be helping one of my own family, and I'll be as hurt as she is when the time comes to hand the baby to a stranger. If I had a husband, I could probably bring it up, but that would be impossible." And she took hold of Pauline's hand to comfort her.

"Does your bloke know you are pregnant Pauline?" Frank was asking now.

"Yes he does, an' he won't let me down. One day he'll come back to us." How she hated her private life being discussed with this man.

57

"Well, if he doesn't, I'd be willing to marry you. So that you can keep the baby of course. You're a very pretty girl, and I could do with some company of an evening."

Pauline felt sick at the thought of living with him, let alone sharing his bed.

"I wouldn't marry you Frank if yer were the last man on earth."

"Pauline! That was very rude. Frank was offering to help you out, and you go and speak to him like that. I'm surprised at you."

"It's alright Molly, it'll be her hormones playing her up. Anyway, I like a girl to say what she thinks." And laughing again he added, "Life wouldn't be dull with her around."

Pauline had had enough, and made an excuse to go and have a lie down in her room, and soon she was fast asleep.

10

Graham, now turned eighteen, had received his call up papers, and Clara was both sad and worried for him. He'd had his birthday only one week ago, and already, they were expecting him to fight. How she wished the war would end. It had seemed a lifetime since everyone had said that it would be over by Christmas, and here they were, two years on, and they were still fighting it out. Mary, missing Ron, didn't want to go out much these days, and Kath had gone home to look after her sick mother. Pauline, she'd heard had gone to stay with an aunt for some reason that no one would tell her. Now her beloved Graham was leaving her too. She was already beginning to feel lonely. Graham had proposed to her on his birthday, and she looked down at the engagement ring on her finger.

"Come back safely my darling," she whispered. She had met his parents of course, and they had welcomed her to the family, so at least she could visit them whilst he was away.

On the day of his leaving, she told him that she couldn't bear to go to the station and watch him go. It would all be too much for her, and Graham had understood what she had meant, but when he had left, she felt guilty, and wondered how she would feel if he never came home and she hadn't kissed him goodbye. She made herself go, and arrived at the platform just as the station master was showing his flag to tell the driver all was safe to move on. The train began to move slowly forward, and she thought that it would be too late to see him, but suddenly, she saw his parents waving into one of the carriages, and she began to shout to them. Thankfully, they heard and she saw them shout to Graham, who looked out of the window, and on seeing her, quickly ran down the train, until he was level with her, and holding out his arm to touch her, he cried, "I love you." And blew a kiss, and she waved until the train was too far in the distance to see him any more. Already she was feeling lonely, and couldn't stop the tears from welling up in her eyes.

Graham had been gone for two weeks, when Clara received a letter from Kathy to say that she would be visiting for the weekend, and would she ask Mary if she fancied a night at the Palais.

"What do you think Mary? It"ll be like old times. I don't know about you, but I could do with a good night out."

"Me too Clara. Yes, write and tell him we're game for it." And at last, the girls had something to look forward to. Clara bought some cheap fabric and ran them both up a dress on her Singer sewing machine, and on the Friday evening, after Kathy had arrived, they spent an hour beautifying themselves. They even lay with a couple of slices of cucumber on their eyes to brighten them. Mary, taking a sneaky look at her mates, burst out laughing when she saw their faces caked in nivea cream, and cucumber stuck over their eyes.

"I wish I had my camera," she said, giggling.

Kathy sat up. "Now look what you've done. My cucumbers fell onto the bed." Feeling around, she couldn't find it anywhere, until Clara sat up, and Mary noticed that it was stuck to her bottom, and laughing again, she pointed to it.

"Well, I'm not putting that back on my face now. Not when I know where it's been." And all three laughed.

It was great to be all together again like this, and as they began to dress, they chatted away none stop. Even Mrs. Gray smiled as she heard them. How nice it was to have laughter in the house again. It had been far too quite of late.

Doing the last bit of fiddling with their hairs, the girls shouted, "Cheerio," and went to catch the tram, but before they had taken half a dozen steps, the air raid alarm went off, and they had to run for shelter instead.

"Bloody Germans. Trust them to pick tonight. Never hear from them all bloody week, and the night we want to go out, they decide to turn up," Mary said feeling fed up, but then she remembered Edna and did a u-turn.

"Where are you off to Mary?" Clara shouted.

"I'm going for Edna. She'll be afraid on her own. You two go on, and we'll come to you."

Seeing Edna cowering in a corner, she was pleased that she had come for her.

"Come on Edna love, let's get you to the shelter."

"I can't Mary. I'll be alright here. You go."

"I'll not leave without you. You"ll be safe with me. Come on." But Mary was crossing her fingers as she said it. She daren't let Edna see that she was nervous too. "It's too dangerous to stay here love. Come on Kathy and Clara will be saving you a seat. It might just be a false alarm, but we don't know that do we?"

"No, but if it isn't, you never know where those bombs will fall. I don't think I could move Mary."

"Yes you can. Hold my hand. That's it, now let's get you standing up. There you go, you did that." And Mary put her arm around her, and said. "We'll have to hurry now Edna. Come on quickly."

Thankfully, Edna did as she was told and the two of them made their way towards the shelter. Seeing Clara's head poking out of the doorway, Mary shouted for her to get inside before she got it blown off, and eventually, she got Edna sitting inside. She had felt Edna shaking with fear, and was glad when someone offered her a drink to calm her.

"Here you are Edna, you have a drop of this brandy with me. It'll do yer good." And she passed it to Edna in a little cup.

"I've got some home made wine here if anyone wants some!" another lady shouted. "And I've got a Guinness. Here yer are, if yer want one!" called out another, and very soon, the shelter was full of people singing. They were singing so loud, that had a bomb been dropped, they wouldn't have heard it. Even Edna was enjoying herself.

"I wish Pauline was here," Kathy said.

"She's safer in Coventry," Edna told her a bit too quickly.

"Safer? You must be joking Edna. Coventry has lots more bombings than we have."

"She'll be fine with my sister."

"Do you think she could come home for the day on Sunday, so I can see her before I go back?"

"I don't think so Kathy. Molly really needs her right now," Edna was hating being questioned, and wished that Kathy would shut up. She was grateful to Mary for coming to help her out.

"Come on girls, leave Edna alone. Can't you see you're worrying her? You'll have her awake all night, wondering if Pauline is going to be alright."

Kathy apologised to Edna, and then added, "Tell her I said hello, will you Edna?"

"I will Kathy, and when she comes back home, I'm sure she'll be pleased to meet up with you."

Mary herself, wondered how Pauline was and had thought it time that she gave her a visit.

11

"Mary! It's great to see yer. I hate it here. I'm bored to death."

"It won't be for much longer Pauline, then you can come home. How far are you now?"

"Seven months, and I feel as fat as a house, I've put on so much weight. Aunt Molly has given me these maternity clothes to wear, but look at 'em Mary. Would you wear anything like this?" And Pauline held up a black skirt with enough elastic in the waist to stretch round three people.

"There not bad Pauline, and they'll do until you've had the baby."

"I wonder how many other poor buggers have worn 'em before me. I know Aunt has laundered them well, but I hate to think how many people have been in 'em."

To change the subject, Mary asked. "Are there any other young people around here you can talk to?"

"No, only the gardener, and he is awful Mary, I wouldn't touch him with a barge pole. Dirty old man he is. He makes me feel sick, but Aunt Molly, thinks the sun shines out of his backside. He keeps asking me to marry him, and Aunt Molly keeps trying to encourage me. He reckons he'll let me keep the baby if I do."

"He can't be that bad, if he says that. Most men wouldn't want it. Perhaps you should think about it."

"No way Mary. I'll keep me baby anyway, I won't let anyone take it away from me."

"How are you going to do that Pauline? Where would you live, and how would you be able to take care of it? You've got to be sensible love. Your Ron doesn't even know yet, and neither do Kathy and Clara. Your Mam wants it to be very hush hush. You can't just turn up with a baby in your arms. It would kill your Mam. It would be different if you were married no one would bother so much then. If I were in your shoes, I'd think about taking up that offer of marriage, even if it's only for your baby's sake."

"But Mary, if yer saw him, yer wouldn't say that. He's awful."

"Come on, he can't be that bad."

"Believe me he is."

"But if he's offering you a home then he can't be that bad. Does he know the baby will be dark skinned?"

"No he doesn't, an' it's none of his business."

"It will be if you marry him."

"Will yer listen, I'm not going to marry anyone apart from my Don."

"Oh well, it's your life, but I don't think you realise how lucky you are. Lots of girls would jump at the chance."

"Let them marry him them."

Feeling guilty for upsetting her mate, Mary put her arm around her shoulders. "I'm sorry Pauline. I didn't come here to make you miserable. I'm supposed to be cheering you up."

"It's not all your fault Mary. I don't know what's the matter with me. One minute I'm up and the next I'm down. I don't half miss Don, and me mates. I don't suppose anyone 'as set eyes on Don have they Mary?"

"I don't think so love. No one has mentioned it if they have."

"He will come back to me Mary, I know he will. That's why I have to keep the baby. He'd hate it if he thought I'd given it away."

Mary would have liked to have said what she thought about that, but thought it best to keep quiet. She didn't want to cause any more upsets. She tried to cheer Pauline up by telling her about the singing they had all done down the air raid shelter, when Kathy had come to visit, but unfortunately, this only made Pauline more miserable.

"I wish I could come home Mary," she said between sobs. "I hate me Mam for sending me away. I thought she loved me."

"You know she does Pauline, that's why she thinks it best that you give the baby up, so that you can have a life."

"I don't want a life without me baby. It's mine, and I want to keep it."

Mary wondered how she could cheer her friend up, and then had an idea.

"Come on Pauline, I'm taking you into town to buy you a new dress. It might make you feel better. I've got a few coupons left, and had a good wage this week, so come on I'll treat you. What do you say?"

"Thanks Mary, but I couldn't let yer spend yer money on me. I know how hard yer have to work for it."

"It's my money Pauline, and if I want to treat you, then I will. Come on, get your coat on, I'll go and tell your Aunt where we are going."

"I'll pay yer back Mary when I go back to work, I promise."

"You'll do no such thing, it's my treat."

"Ok, and thanks Mary yer a good friend."

The town was almost empty, when they arrived, which meant that they could have a leisurely stroll, without being poked and prodded. Mary had told molly that they would eat out, and so there was no rush to get back.

The sun was out, but there was also a small breeze making it feel comfortable.

Finding a baby shop, Pauline couldn't take her eyes off of all the baby outfits, and unaware of what she was doing, began to stroke her belly. Seeing a beautiful green pram with a cream sun canopy, she couldn't help giving out a loud ahh! It was standing proudly in the centre of the shop, and draped over it were blankets in pastel colours, and a lovely lemon cover made from a satin fabric. Around the sides it had a frill in matching fabric, and there was even a pillow case to match. She imagined how she would feel pushing it along the streets, with her darling baby inside, and was even more determined to keep her child.

Mary saw the longing in her eyes, and began to feel guilty for bringing her to a shop like this, but she had no idea where else they could go to. She tried to bring Pauline back to reality, and asked.

"Seen a dress you like yet Pauline?"

"I haven't really looked Mary. I suppose we'd better ask what they have."

The young girl behind the counter was very helpful, without being pushy, and got out several dresses for Pauline to look at. "When's your baby due?" she asked Pauline.

"In two months."

"Oh not too long to wait then? We have just had some new baby clothes in if you'd like to see them. I could get them out of the stock room if you're interested?"

"Not today thanks," Mary butted in. "Perhaps another time. We've just come for the dress today."

"Certainly madam. Was there any particular colour you wanted?"

"I like this blue one, but it depends on how much it costs because my friend is treating me, and I don't want to be greedy." It was a pretty dress, made of cotton, and with the pleats hanging from a yolk at the top of the bodice, it would hide Pauline's stomach lovely. It was much nicer than the skirts that she was having to wear now.

"If that's the one you like, then that's the one you shall have. We'll take it please," She told the assistant.

After lunch, Mary told Pauline that it was time that she caught the train for home, and Pauline gave her a hug, and thanked her once again.

Molly thought the dress was beautiful and told her so.

"Put it on Pauline and let me see it on you." And when Pauline had it on, Molly gasped, for the dress suited Pauline admirably, and she couldn't help but keep telling her so. When Pauline was about to take it off, there suddenly came a wolf whistle through the window. Frank was about to tell Molly that he had finished what he had been doing, when he spotted Pauline in the dress.

"Lord above, I never thought you could look any prettier than you do, but in that dress, you like a film star. It would make a good dress to get married in you know. The offer is still open when you're ready." Frank could feel the saliva filling his mouth as he visualised her being his bride, and taking her to his bed. She'd certainly be something to brag about to his drinking mates. He wished she'd hurry up and say yes. He didn't feel he could wait for much longer. There were times when he felt he'd have to take her there and then, but knew that wouldn't be good for him. She had to come to him willingly.

The sight of him made Pauline feel nauseous, but then she could hear Mary's words going around in her head. You will be allowed to keep your baby. It will be worth it. It"ll only be until Don can fetch you. All these thoughts were making her giddy, and without real thought, she asked him.

"If I marry yer, yer'll promise I can keep me baby?"

Frank couldn't believe what he'd heard. Of course he didn't want the baby, but if it meant having Pauline, then he'd have to put up with it.

"Well, I'm waiting for yer answer."

"Scout's honour, you can keep it."

"Put that in writing," Pauline was telling Frank now.

"What?"

"You heard, I said put it in writing, or the deal's off."

"Alright, just as you wish. Pass me a pen and I will."

Molly hadn't been able to speak from surprise until now, and she had to ask Pauline.

"Have you thought this through Pauline? You need to be very sure, it's a big step to take, and what's done can't be undone quickly."

"My Mam will let me keep me baby if I wed won't she Aunt Molly?"

"I'm pretty sure she will love, but naturally I'll have to ask her."

"Then if she says yes, I will marry Frank."

Frank stepped forward for a cuddle, but Pauline brushed him aside, and told him. "Me Mam hasn't said yes yet, so don't go getting any ideas beyond yer station yet."

"I can wait Pauline m'dear, I can wait. There'll be lots of time for cuddles when we're married."

Pauline almost heaved in front of him, but managed to hold it back. She felt that she must be going mad to offer to marry this man whom she loathed so much, but for the sake of her baby, she would do it.

Arrangements for the marriage were made for as quickly as was possible, and it was to be held at the Leicester Registry Office, as that was more convenient for her Mam to get to. Pauline had said that she only want a few guests, as it was a marriage of convenience. Mary had been asked to let Kathy and Clara know the truth, and they both felt very sad for Pauline. Instead of a joyous wedding, it would be quite sombre. Fancy having to marry someone you didn't love, just because you were pregnant, and they couldn't believe how Don had treated her so badly. Even they thought he was made of better stuff than that.

Clara had already begun to knit baby matinee coats, and all three of the girls decided that they must buy something for when it was born, and took it in turns to come up with ideas. Finally, they decided on a wicker cradle, and would put a couple of blankets into it, plus a tin of baby talc.

BUTTON NOSE

Clara was growing excited about the birth. "I can't wait to hold it," she cried, and then she asked if Frank didn't mind about the baby being dark skinned.

"He doesn't know yet," Mary told her.

"What?! He'll throw her out when he knows, won't he?"

"Pauline has sworn me to secrecy until it's born, so I can't tell him. Her Mam doesn't even know yet, and Ron doesn't even know she's pregnant. I hate deceiving them all like this, but it's Pauline's wishes and not mine."

"I wouldn't like to be in your shoes Mary when they find out. You'll be in hot water for not telling."

"I know and I feel so guilty, I don't know who to please. Them or Pauline."

"Well I think it's time you looked after yourself. Pauline got herself into this mess, it's up to her to get herself out of it. I think it's your duty to let Ron know everything. Why should you ruin your future for the sake of someone else's?"

"I have thought about that a lot, but honest Clara, I don't know what to do for the best. I've kept this secret for so long, it's been helpful to unburden myself by talking about it."

"You should have told us earlier, and we could have sorted it together. The longer you leave off telling him, the worse it'll be for you."

"I know you're right. I've got some serious thinking to do haven't I?"

"Yes, and the sooner the better."

Putting her new blue dress over her head, Pauline was too depressed to care if her hair was messed or not. She had been dreading her wedding day. This should be the happiest day of her life, and it would have been had it been Don she was marrying, but Frank? How was she supposed to grit her teeth and carry on as though she loved him? It was taking her all her time not to cry, and if it wasn't for the sake of keeping her baby, she would have been thrilled to call the wedding off.

She stroked her stomach and tried to reassure her baby. "I'll do anything for yer my darlin' even this because I love yer so much an' want to take care of yer. I won't let anyone hurt yer. I love yer now an' I'll always love yer, just like yer Daddy will when he sees yer. He loves me too my darlin' and one day he'll come back to us, yer've got to believe me, but until that time, we've got to be very brave, and do what has to be done right now, an' I'm willin' to do that for yer."

"Aren't you ready yet Pauline?" Molly asked as she came into Pauline's room. "We'll have to hurry if you want to get there in time, or everyone will think your not coming. Come on, let me help you." And Molly began to button up the buttons at the back of her dress, before picking up a comb to put through Pauline's hair.

"Help me Aunt Molly, please?" Pauline begged.

"I'm trying to if only you'd stand still."

"I mean help me through this day. It's going to be very hard for me."

"I understand how you might be feeling, but it is kind of Frank to marry you. He didn't have to offer you know. And after the wedding, you"ll only be living a few doors away from me, so you can often come and visit me, and I can help you with the baby. I don't think you realise what a lucky girl you are."

Pauline didn't agree that living with greasy Frank was lucky, but she said nothing. How she would let him make love to her, was anyone's guess, and hoped that being pregnant would put him off for a while.

At the Registry Office, Pauline didn't feel as excited about the affair as her guests seemed to be. Her heart was as heavy as lead as she began to walk towards the registrar. Frank was by her side, and she could smell the sweat from his uncared for body.

Looking at his wife to be, Frank was already thinking ahead to the night time, and couldn't wait for it to arrive. Fancy him bedding a beautiful girl like Pauline! Never in his wildest dreams would he have thought it would happen to him. He looked at her now, but saw through the beautiful dress she was wearing, and he was imagining her young soft body, and how it would feel next to his. It was a shame that she was pregnant, but had she not been, he would never have had this chance of marrying her. Anyway, he wouldn't let the little brat interfere with his life. He would have to come first in his house, and the babby, would be way down the list for attention. Naturally, he hadn't yet told Pauline that. He had to get her to marry him first, then the rest would come later.

The registrar couldn't help noticing how far Pauline's pregnancy had gone. Even the pleats of the dress could not hide the fullness of her belly, and she guessed that this was only a marriage of convenience, but it was of no business of hers, and she began to take the service. She couldn't help noticing that Frank was more for it than Pauline, and she began to feel sorry for the girl. When it came to the part of the service when she had to ask if anyone thought that they shouldn't be married, she half expected all the guests to shout I do, but not one of them stood up, even though she waited for a reply longer than was normal. She was about to proceed, when the door was flung open, and a young man rushed in shouting.

"Stop this marriage. I'm not too late am I?"

The registrar felt the same relief that Pauline was feeling, and when she ran into the man's arms she wondered if he were the babies father, but then heard someone in the crowd refer to him as Pauline's brother.

"Oh Ron, it's great to see yer, but yer can't stop the wedding. I'll have to give me baby away if yer do."

"No you won't, and you're coming home. Thank God I was able to get here in time. Mary and I will help you to bring up the baby, won't we Mary?"

"I'll be glad to Ron, and thanks for coming. How did you get the leave?"

"I did a swap with a mate." And turning back to Pauline, he said, "Come on our kid, let's have you home where you belong."

"Yer don't understand Ron, I can't come home, the baby will be black." There was aloud gasp from the guests, but the biggest one came from Frank.

"You little bitch. You never told me that."

"Well, she's telling you now, and I don't care if the baby is black, green or blue, it's my niece or nephew, and I say she is still coming home. Do you hear that Mam?"

"Yes Ron, I hear you."

"Good. Come on then we don't want to stay here any longer, let's go?"

Pauline began to cry from relief, and hugged her brother as close as was possible under the circumstances. "I love yer, our Ronnie, I love yer for doing this for me, an' I'll never forget it."

As they all left, Frank was heard to mutter, "A black bastard. She was going to let me bring up a black bastard."

Edna didn't speak much until they arrived home, and then, pulling Ron to one side, she asked. "What the hell possessed you to do that our Ron? Now what are we going to do?"

"Do? Nothing Mam, except be there for Pauline. She needs us more than ever now. Why the hell did you send her away like that? If Mary hadn't let me know, then Pauline's life would have been ruined."

"Well, it'll be more ruined now you've brought her home, and all of ours for that matter. I had no idea that she was having a black baby. It gets worse. I don't know what we'll do. I won't dare to hold my head up any more."

"Yes you will Mam. Who do you care most about. Pauline or the neighbours?"

"Pauline of course. You know I do."

"Then show her. She is carrying your grandchild. Could you live with yourself knowing that you had told her to give it away?"

"Looking at it like that, I suppose I couldn't."

"Well then, did I do the right thing or not?"

"Yes you did son, and I'm sorry. It's hard making decisions with no one to ask if it's right or wrong. I don't know if Pauline will ever forgive me."

"She will Mam, especially when she sees how sorry you are."

Mary was talking to Pauline in her bedroom. "I'm sorry I didn't keep my word to you Pauline. About telling Ron I mean. I felt that he had a right to know what was happening to you. Can you forgive me?"

"Forgive yer? I'm bloody grateful to yer Mary. If our Ron hadn't have stopped the wedding, I'd have been married to Frank now. It's the best thing yer could've done for me." And Pauline gave her mate a hug.

"Can anyone join in?" Ron asked as he came to the door with Edna.

"Cause yer can. The more the merrier."

"Does that include me Pauline?"

"Of course Mam. I'm sorry for all the trouble I've caused yer."

"I'm sorry too Pauline. I should have stuck by you like a mother should."

"It's ok Mam, it all came out ok, and I'm really happy to be home again."

12

If that bloody alarm goes off tonight Mary, I'll bloody scream. Three nights with hardly any sleep is no joke," Clara said, buttoning her suspender to the last pair of nylons she had been given by Pauline. She had saved them for this weekend, when Graham was home on leave.

"Yeah! I wouldn't mind if they were all genuine, but the last few have all been false alarms. They can't get anything right can they. I swear they do it to annoy us. I can just imagine them saying. Let's get the buggers out of their beds."

"Well, they hadn't better do it tonight whilst I'm having a cuddle with my Graham. I can't wait to see him. My hearts pounding like the devil with the excitement."

Mary laughed. "You'd better…." She stopped suddenly as Mrs Gray sounded to be in distress over something, and the girls ran down to see what was the matter.

Mrs. Gray looked ashen as she held out the telegram to Clara. She knew that these things could only mean bad news, and she feared that something had happened to Graham. She pulled up a chair for Clara to sit down on. "What is it? What's it say Clara?" she inquired, but all Clara could do was to pass it over to Mary.

"I can't do it Mary. You open it."

Taking it from her, Mary opened it with trembling fingers, and as she read the message, she wondered how Clara would react.

"Tell me what it says Mary?"

"I'm sorry Clara. It says that Graham is missing. Never returned from the mission he was on."

"No! that can't be right. Read it again Mary, there must be some mistake. He's coming home today. He told me he was.

I'm going to meet him. I'd better get me coat, or I'll miss him and he'll think I'm not going."

"It's not a mistake Clara, they wouldn't send these things out for fun love."

Clara began to cry. "There's got to be a mistake. I can't live without him. He can't be dead Mary, he just can't be."

"It doesn't say he's dead Clara, only missing. He might turn up, or he could have been captured. They'll let you know as soon as they hear anything."

Mrs. Gray poured out a tot of brandy for them all, and eventually Clara managed to stop crying.

"You're right Mary. I know he's not dead, because he swore he'd never leave me. If he was I'd know it in my heart wouldn't I? Women know these sort of things."

"That's right Clara, and if he's been captured, well he'll be back home as soon as the war is over."

"Dear Lord, let that be quick."

Would you like to sleep in my room with me tonight Clara? It'll be better than you being alone."

"Yes please Mary."

They didn't get much sleep, because Clara was tossing and turning all night, and Mary moved into an armchair to give her more space. She couldn't help wondering how she would cope if she received a telegram about Ron. This war was unbearable. It wasn't only the boys fighting that were getting hurt, but relatives at home also, even if it was only emotionally. It still left scars to cope with.

The next morning, Mary was telling Edna and Pauline the bad news, and Pauline wanted to go and see Clara, but Mary told her that she was still sleeping. Whether it was shock or not, no one was sure, but suddenly Pauline was doubled over with pains in her stomach, and when her waters broke, Edna knew that it was time to call an ambulance. The labour lasted for three hours, and when little Louise Emily entered the world, Pauline couldn't stop looking at her. She was so beautiful, and had her daddy's eyes, which only showed momentarily before being closed again. Her skin was lighter than Don's, but she also had his nose. Pauline bent to kiss her daughter, and told her, "I love you so much my precious little button nose. You are so like your daddy. He will love you to bits when he sees you." Louise snuggled further towards Pauline's body. After feeding her, Pauline wrapped her tightly into the white blanket that had been placed across the metal cot, and put her down to sleep.

Edna had been allowed a glimpse of her new grandchild, and even she had to admit what a beauty she was. She felt very proud of being a grandma, and couldn't wait to tell everyone all about her.

13

Graham felt a hard nudge in his ribs, made by the butt of the German soldier's gun. Several other prisoners received the same treatment, if they weren't moving fast enough, but Graham wasn't one to bite his tongue.

"Who the hell do you think you're pushing?" he shouted loudly, and in return, Graham was given a mouth of abuse, and pushed again. "Do that again, and I'll give you my fist," he told the man.

"Come on quickly, you don't want to lose your head do you?" A prisoner at the side of him took hold of his arm to get him to go onto the train. "They'll shoot you rather than look at you, if they take a dislike to you. Best to hold your mouth and say nothing." Thankful now that Graham was heeding what he was saying, they both climbed into a carriage, which was already so overcrowded that they felt suffocated. "I'm Bill by the way," he said trying his hardest to stretch his hand out towards Graham.

"Thanks. I'm Graham. I swear I'd have knocked him senseless if you hadn't brought me to me senses. Who the hell do they think they are, treating us like that?"

"I feel like you Graham, but I'd prefer to be pushed, than have a hole in my head. Have you anyone special back home?"

"Yes I have a girlfriend. How about you?"

"Yes, I do too. If we concentrate our minds onto them, instead of these bastards, it will keep us from doing something daft."

"Yes ok. She'll be worried sick when she hears. I'm supposed to be at home this weekend."

"What happened?"

"I was just about to finish my stint, when we got ambushed from behind. We tried to break free, but when they began firing guns, we had no choice but to let them have us. How about you?"

"I was…."

Bill didn't get to tell him because they were shouted at to be quiet, and as the train began to move, they all seemed to fall backwards with the jolt, squashing each other even more.

It was a long journey, as the train pulled into sidings many times to let other trains pass, and once in a while the men were let out to go to the toilet, which was done up the sides of the train.

Graham was glad for a pee. He'd found it difficult to hold it, and noticed several of the men had already wet themselves on the train making it stink with urine. He began to wonder if there was a chance of an escape, but the soldier who had nudged him, was watching him closely, as though reading his mind, and he decided he'd better wait for the next stop. Naturally, the next was no better than the last, and Graham had no other choice, but to get back on to the train with the others.

When the train came to it's final stop, the prisoners were told to get off, and were ushered into the back of a big army lorry, which took them to a camp in Germany. Glad to stretch their legs, Bill and Graham jumped down and looked around them. Several other prisoners were standing around to see who their new buddies were.

Graham and Bill were taken to one of the wooden huts which had bunk beds two or three high. They were pleased that they were kept together, and Graham threw himself onto the top of a double bunk, whilst bill preferred the lower.

"Ouch!" Graham shouted as his back hit the hardness of his mattress. "You'd think they'd have put a few feathers in it. After all, they knew they were having guests. How very inconsiderate of them."

Bill laughed loudly.

"Do you think they have a clubhouse? I could do with a pint right now," Graham said, looking over the side of his bunk and into Bills.

"You'll be lucky mate." A voice from a bunk further up the room, made them turn to see where it had come from, and walking over to the man, Bill asked.

"Been here long?"

"Too bloody long! About a year I reckon. It's hard to keep count of the months in here. It's hard, but you don't have to let that lot know it, or they don't leave you alone. I'm Frederick by the way." He said holding out his hand to them.

"Hello Frederick, I'm Bill, and this is Graham. Have you ever thought of escaping?"

"Of course I have, and I've tried, but you always get caught and brought back again. If you ever do think about doing it, you must let the escape committee know first, in case they have something big on for that night."

"Who are they?"

"You'll meet 'em in time. I can't say any more than that. Ok?"

"We understand Frederick."

"Good! Call me Fred by the way. Fredericks only for Sundays."

Hearing a cheer from outside, Graham had a look through the window to see what it was all about, and saw some of the prisoners playing football. He watched for a while, and when he was about to turn round again, someone leaning against a wall caught his eye. At first, he thought that his eyes were deceiving him, but no, they weren't, he was sure it was him, and he walked outside for a closer look. As he grew closer, he couldn't help but notice how the man had changed. no longer the strong body he once was, but now thin and gaunt, and his face long and drawn. The eyes, once bright and playful were now only dead and empty.

"Cigarette mate?" he asked passing one over to the man, but the man seemed not to have heard, so Graham lit one up for him and shoved it into his mouth. "Don't I know you?" he asked him. Still no reaction, but Graham carried on speaking. "I think I saw you at the Palais with my girl's friend Pauline." At last there was a flicker of interest. "Your baby she's having is it? I've heard that she's still hoping that you will return to marry her. Her Mam told her she had to have it adopted, but you know how stubborn Pauline is. Wouldn't think of it, and even agreed to marry some nut so's she could keep it."

"Married. Pauline?"

"No. Her brother Ron fetched her home to have your baby. So, will you go back when this is all behind us?"

"Back? Yes." And for the first time of speaking to him, Graham noticed a flicker of light in his eye. Perhaps this was news that he needed to bring him back into the real world.

14

Pauline was getting excited about Louise's forthcoming birthday. She could hardly believe that the two years had passed so quickly. The war was still raging, and she'd had no news of Don, and yet she still believed that he would be back for them both. She knew from Clara that Graham had been a prisoner since the birth of Louise, and that he was alright, but she hoped that Don was still safe somewhere, wherever he was.

Louise was adored by everyone who had met her. She seemed to grow more delightful with each year. Edna was an excellent grandma, and was always willing to mind her for Pauline. Secretly, Edna felt so guilty for almost losing her for good, that she tried to make up for it by spoiling Louise, which wasn't a difficult thing to do, seeing as her little granddaughter had the loveliest of natures. Always smiling and happy. Very rarely would she cry or sulk, and having her in the house had given them all so much joy. Edna was so pleased that Ron had come home and made her see sense. There had been times when she had heard the odd person make a remark on having a black baby, but Edna had become brave, and had told them, "As long as you don't have to look after her, what business is it of yours?" And they had scuttled away well reprimanded.

Pauline was playing her usual games with Louise before putting her to bed. She had just given her a bath, and was trying to put a towel around her body, but Louise was having none of it, and ran away giggling.

"I shall come to get you!" Pauline called out to her, knowing that this was what Louise wanted her to do. It was the same thing every night, but Pauline still went along with it. She adored playing with her daughter.

As Louise hid behind a chair, Pauline crept along on her hands and knees telling Louise that she was getting nearer and nearer. Louise, could hardly breathe for laughing, and when Pauline managed to grab her, she squealed with delight.

Edna loved to watch them both. She had seen it every night, and probably would see it all again, but she never tired of seeing it. Louise's laugh was so funny that you couldn't help but smile.

Picking Louise up into her arms, Pauline told her. "You wait 'til yer daddy comes, he'll catch yer, and he'll kiss you all over like this." And she began to kiss her daughter all over, making her laugh more.

"No, Daddy no," she told Pauline, "Daddy not catch."

"You shouldn't tell her that Pauline," Edna scalded. It's not right to build a child's hopes up like that. We both know that her daddy isn't coming back. It's been too long now. We won't be seeing him again."

"He will Mam, I know he will. You've never met him, so yer don't know what he's like. When this rotten war is over, he'll be back. I'm sure of it, an' I don't want him to be a stranger to Louise when he does."

"Oh well, if you know it, there's no point in me saying anything. I just hope that Louise doesn't get hurt, when she realises there is no daddy. There'll be lots of daddies that won't come home, and hers will be one of them."

"Daddy home?" Louise said, pulling Pauline's face round to face her.

"Of course daddy will be home my little button nose," Pauline reassured her, and laughed when Louise rubbed her nose.

Dressed in her nightdress, Louise fetched a book for her mummy to read to her, and then she climbed up to sit next to her, so that she could see the pictures in it. Pauline had only read a couple of pages when she felt Louise's head heavy against her arm, and looking down, she saw that Louise had fallen asleep. Picking her up, she carried her up the stairs to put her into her cot. She looked down at her sleeping peacefully, and thought her a little miracle. How glad she was that she and Don had made this beautiful baby together. "You were meant to be, my darling," she whispered before turning off the light, and going back down the stairs to Edna, where she began to wrap the little gifts that she had bought for Louise's birthday. Edna was making some jellies from jelly crystals she'd had in the pantry. "I've got some spam for the sandwiches Pauline, and Ivy on the Checketts Road gave me three eggs, so I can hard boil those as well."

"That should do Mam thanks. Clara and Mary are going to bring something, and Mary said she'd made a cake as well."

"How is Clara?"

"Ok, but naturally she worries about Graham. But at least he's alive."

"Yes, at least she knows that much, but they don't get much food in those places. It won't be easy when the men come home. I remember after the last war, how hard it was for them to adjust after being away for so long. Women at home had become independent and the men didn't like that at all. They had been used to ruling the roost, and it caused a lot of arguments. They expect their women to be at home in the kitchen."

"It won't be easy for the women then. They won't like that after having the freedom of working."

When Pauline had finished wrapping her presents, she placed them onto the table ready for Louise to see in the morning.

Pauline was awake early on the morning of Louise's birthday, and she waited patiently for her daughter to stir. Normally it was the other way around, and Louise would wake her mummy, but of course today, she had decided to sleep a bit longer. It was another half an hour before Pauline heard her moving about, and she reached over to sit her up.

"Happy Birthday button nose," she said kissing Louise on top of her head. Louise, rubbed her eyes and looked around, and seeing Pauline, she gave her a big smile. "Come on sunshine, let's go downstairs and give yer some breakfast, and then we can wake Nanna up so she can watch yer open yer cards and presents."

At first, Louise was still too sleepy to say much, but when she was sitting in her high chair, she suddenly came alive.

"Lou-Lou's birthday Mummy?" she asked, bending her head over to one side to look Pauline in the face.

"Yes darlin' it's Louise's birthday, and when yer've eaten yer breakfast, yer can open yer cards."

Edna had heard them talking down stairs, and got up herself, so as not to miss the excitement. "Happy Birthday my little precious one." And she bent to kiss her granddaughter.

After Louise had finished her meal, Pauline lifted her out of her chair and put her down onto the floor, and then she gave Louise her birthday cards to open. Louise was too excited to open them slowly, and began tearing the envelopes, almost tearing the cards with them.

"Take yer time Louise," Pauline scalded, but Louise wasn't listening, and one by one, she pulled out the cards to look at them, and each one that she pulled out, she held up for her Mam and Nanna to see. Pauline stood each one onto the sideboard, and then she passed Louise her presents. Pauline had made her a dress in pink cotton, with white lace around the collar and cuffs. Louise was thrilled with it, and held it to her and began to dance around with it, making her mum and Nan smile at her. Edna had bought her a couple of colouring books and crayons, and after Louise was dressed, she lay flat out on her tummy, on top of the rug in front of the fire to do some colouring, and each time she showed Edna her picture that she'd coloured, Edna told her that they were beautiful, but she couldn't help smiling as each picture was hidden by the scribble of crayons all over it.

In the afternoon, Pauline put Louise up for a rest whilst she helped to get the table ready for the party. Edna had given her one of her best tablecloths, and on top of that, Pauline had placed the cups, and plates, whilst Edna wrapped up the cutlery into some white serviettes that she'd had since before the war had begun.

Hearing a tap on the window, Pauline turned to see Clara and Mary, and went to let them in.

"Where is she?" Mary asked, looking around the room.

"Having a nap, so she won't be tired for the party."

"We'll put her presents on the table shall we?"

"Yeah! Thanks both of yer for coming."

"Do you mind if we put the radio on Edna?"

"Of course you can Mary, but not too loud, we don't want her up yet until we've finished setting the table. I've brought the cake Pauline. Sorry it's not decorated or anything, but you can't get the sugar these days."

"It's lovely Mary, and thoughtful of yer to do it for us." The sound of Glenn miller was coming from the radio, and they all began to sing, with the occasional dance in between. Then suddenly, the radio went very quiet, they thought at first, that the electricity had gone, but when a man spoke to say there was to be an announcement by the Prime Minister, they listened carefully.

Winston Churchill, coughed, before telling everyone that the war in Europe would end officially, at twelve o'clock midnight. He then said that they must now end the war in Japan.

Edna sat down with a flop. Whilst the girls stood staring at each other until it registered.

"The war is over! The bloody war, it's over girls!" and they all began to scream and cheer. Soon after, the street was alive with noisy neighbours, shouting to each other, and flags began to fly out of windows. Someone even brought out a piano, and began to play it in the street, and people crowded around it singing as loudly as they possibly could, which awoke Louise, but Pauline didn't mind, and fetched her out to join in the fun.

Happy Birthday Mary sang to her, and then added that it would be the best one ever. Louise had no idea what was going on, but she was having a good time any way, and when she began to sing, "Happy birfday me," she made them all laugh.

Returning in doors for her party, Mary and Clara handed over their presents. Mary had given her a little black doll, and Clara had given her a book of nursery rhymes., and then Mary went out into the garden where she had hidden a special present, and when she brought it inside, Pauline gasped, and Louise tried to climb into it.

"It's beautiful Mary, but yer shouldn't have gone to that expense."

"I didn't Pauline. It's from Ron. He's been down our shed on his leaves making it for her for a surprise, and he asked me to give it to her today."

Pauline almost cried. She felt so lucky to have him for her brother. She looked closer at the cot, which was painted in yellow paint, and he'd even put some farmyard animals onto it. Thinking it was for her, Louise was almost inside it, and Edna had to take her out of it.

"It's not for you Louise. Look! It's for your dolly." Edna picked up her new dolly, put it inside the cot, and covered it with the cover that Mary had made for it. Louise loved it, and was very quiet as she played with it, her little tongue sticking out of the corner of her mouth as she concentrated. It took Pauline a lot of encouragement, before she could get her to come to the table to eat, because she'd rather play with her dolly.

Suddenly, Edna began to cry.

"Mam! What's the matter?"

"Nothing love. I was just thinking what a day today has been. It's been the best for many a year."

"You never know what tomorrow is going to bring do you?" Clara added. "Do you think my Graham will be home this week?"

"I don't know Clara. I shouldn't think that they'll keep them for too long now, especially after being in a camp." Edna replied. "I wonder if they have heard the news yet?"

"If they are, they'll all be as happy as we are, I shouldn't wonder. I can't wait to see him again." Then looking at her mates, she asked. "What shall we do tonight? Go to town?"

"I'm game Clara. What about you Pauline, are you coming?"

"I'd love to, but I couldn't take our Louise, I bet there'll be crowds there."

"Don't be silly Pauline, you can leave her with me. You go and enjoy yourself."

"What about you Mam. Don't you want to go to the club or something?"

"No love. I did it after the last war, now it's your turn."

"Oh thanks Mam, I love yer."

Edna couldn't understand why, after she had nearly made her give Louise away. Pauline was a good mother, and they both had come to love Louise dearly.

The town was filled with people from all walks of life, and they didn't give a toss with whom they were dancing, because they were too happy to care. Soldiers on leave were being kissed by girls, and Mary, Pauline and Clara, joined in the conga that was being danced around the Clock Tower. Ale was being drunk by far too many, and many folk ended up in casualty as they stumbled and broke bones, keeping ambulances and nurses very busy.

The gaieties carried on until the early hours of the morning, and it was a tired threesome that arrived home afterwards.

"I'd invite yer for a drink, but I'm too tired," Pauline told the others.

"Thanks Pauline, but I couldn't drink another thing. I'm so tired, I think I'll sleep until the cows come home," Clara answered.

"Me too," Mary told them, hardly able to walk straight. It was good though wasn't it?"

"Yeah!" the others replied laughing.

There were still some neighbours in the street celebrating, but Pauline was pleased to get in home and kick off her shoes. She had no idea how she made it up the stairs, but somehow, she had got herself into bed.

15

"Bill, listen! What's all that commotion? There must be something going on, there's such a palaver out there."

"I can hear it Graham, let's go and see."

There was so much shouting, that at first it was difficult to hear what anyone was saying. It was very hard to concentrate these days any way, due to lack of food and sleep. The only time that they received a real treat was when the Red Cross called with food parcels. All of the prisoners were very thin, and bones showed through their skins. It was a wonder they could stand at all. Many was the times that weary prisoners were having to be held upright at roll call by their mates, so that the German soldiers couldn't see how ill they were.

Assuming now, that his imagination was playing tricks on him, Graham listened carefully, then realising that it wasn't he began to shout with the other prisoners.

"It's over Bill, the stinking war is over. We're going home mate." And grabbing Bill by the arms they danced around shouting loudly, "We bloody won!" and they put two fingers up to the German men. "That's to you and yours," Graham told them. Then seeing Don looking dazed by all of the noise, he went over to him. "Hear that Don? We're all going home. Soon you will see your Pauline again." He had taken care of Don since seeing how the war had effected him. Something really bad must have made him like this. Perhaps he'd seen a friend killed, or he'd been shot himself. Who could tell? Many men had come out of it the same way that Don had, and it would take a lot of help for them to recover.

The prison gates were opened up, but the prisoners were told to await the arrival of army lorries to fetch them. It seemed that it was mainly the Germans who were running through the gates, and Graham and Bill went to search for food.

Pauline's head was throbbing from drinking the night before, and she was pleased that Louise hadn't woke early. She was grateful to her Mam, who brought her in a cup of tea.

"Have a good night love?" Edna asked.

"Too good Mam, I think my head will burst soon, but it was all worth it. I wish yer could have been there with us, and our Ron. I've never seen so many people around the clock tower, and they were all singing and dancing. I still can't believe the war is over, can you?"

"No, but it is, and that's brilliant news, but it won't help the women who've lost their men. It will hurt a lot when they see the others coming home, knowing that theirs won't."

"Do yer think Don is alright Mam?"

Edna was pleased that Louise was beginning to stir, and pretending not to have heard Pauline, she picked her up. "Are you coming down stairs with your Nanna, so that Mummy can go back to sleep for a bit longer?" And she carried Louise out of the room, leaving Pauline to relax on her pillow. She couldn't stop thinking about Don. She had been waiting for so long. Would he love his daughter? Will he be disappointed because she wasn't a son? Her Mam didn't believe that he would come back to her, but Pauline knew this would not be so. It was as though someone, somewhere was telling her to believe in him, and she did.

That evening, there was to be a big street party, and everyone was buzzing with excitement, as all offered to give a hand, be it set out tables which had been borrowed from the local adult school, or trimming the street with banners. Even the children were painting Union Jack's onto white paper to trim the tables with. Paper hats came out of hiding places in cupboards, and lofts, and plates were borrowed from several houses. Jellies and trifles had been made, and hens were cooked. Even the side of a pig was brought out to be roasted. It seemed like a good spread, compared to what they had been used to eating. Women were hoping that food would no longer be rationed, and were looking forward to some delicacies.

The children, all seated now, were offered sandwiches, but Louise was asking,   "Mummy, jelly please?" holding out a dish for it.

"Not yet Louise, you have some bread first, there's a good girl."

"Oh go on. Give her jelly if she wants it. It's a party."

Pauline recognised the voice instantly and turning around, she threw her arms around his neck.

"Ron! Oh Ron, it's great to see yer."

"Perhaps I should go away more often if it gets a welcome like that," he told her laughing.

"Don't yer dare."

Bending down to Louise, Ron asked her if she had a kiss for him.

A little shy at first, Louise hesitated , then lifting her face to his, she gave him one, leaving butter on his lips. Ron laughed and wiped it off, and then asked where his Mam was.

"Still in home, but she'll be out soon. She'll be dead pleased to see yer."

"I'll go and catch her before she does. She's bound to want to ask a lot of questions. Any news on Graham?"

"Not yet, but it shouldn't be long now."

"Right. I'm off to see Mam now, but I'll be out for a pint myself soon."

"And quite welcome you'll be lad, after what you've done for us." One of the women told him, and other's agreed with her. As he was walking towards home, they all began to sing.

For he's a jolly good fellow, and before going indoors, he turned and saluted to them, making them cheer loudly.

Edna was thrilled to see him. "Oh son, it's great to see you. It's nice to have you home safe and sound. Have you seen Mary?"

"Not yet Mam. I can't wait to surprise her."

"I can just imagine her face. She's been on hot coals, wondering when you'll be home. Will you both be going in to the street?"

"Too right we will. I wouldn't miss it for the world. Any more of me mates home yet?"

"Quite a few." Michael up the road is home, and Tommy, oh and Eric. I expect you'll see them all at the do." Muriel at no three, was saying how happy their mothers were to have the boys home, and I'm feeling the same now that your home. Now you get off and see Mary, or someone will tell her before you can surprise her."

"Right then, I'll just take my things up stairs out of your way, and I'll be off. I want to ask her to marry me Mam."

"Oh Ron, I hope she says yes. She's a lovely girl. What a good week this is turning out to be. Before you go Ron, I've got something I need to say to you. I want to say thank you for bringing our Pauline home to have the baby. I was thinking of myself as usual, and what the neighbours would think, but now I know, it's not important what they think. It's Pauline that counts. I don't think I could have lived with myself, knowing I'd made her give our Louise away. She's the best thing to happen to us for years. If you hadn't have come home that day, then I'd never have got to know her, and I'd have missed a lot of happiness I've had with the child. Pauline has forgiven me, but I've no idea how she could. I don't think I would have been so forgiving if it had been me."

"Yes you would Mam, you and Pauline are alike as two peas in a pod, and I'm sure you've made up for the upset by accepting Louise. I wish that Don would come home. It would make her life perfect then."

"Do you think he will Ron? I can't see it myself. It's been a long time."

"Who knows. You just have to hope don't you? Do you mind him being black?"

"Not if he comes back and is good to Pauline. She deserves some happiness. She has given up so much to look after Louise. I know how hard it is not to have a man to help you."

"Well, we are all proud of you Mam. You've not done a bad job. You only have to look at me to see how handsome you've made me."

Edna laughed. "Get off with you. There's nothing like loving yourself is there eh?"

"Well, if I don't say it, nobody else will! I'm off to Mary's now. Keep your fingers crossed that she says yes."

"I will son. I will. Let me know as soon as you have something to tell."

"Come in and wait. I won't be long Pauline!" Mary shouted when a knock came at her door. "You know how long it takes me to get ready." And without turning, she shouted, "Sit down will you. I've almost finished!"

"Where? Here, or here?" Ron asked, sitting as close to her as he could, and Mary, hardly able to believe her ears, spun round.

"Oh my God Ron. It's you! I can't believe it. It's you!"

"It's me alright, or it was the last time I looked at me face. Come here and let me kiss you." They both clung to each other, and Ron told her. "I've waited so long for this moment. I love you so much Mary. More than you"ll ever know."

"Me too Ron, me too."

Going down onto one knee, Ron asked her. "Will you marry me Mary?"

"Of course I will, and I'll be proud to do so."

Taking a little box from his pocket, Ron opened it to show Mary the diamond ring that he had bought, and after placing it onto her finger, he kissed her again.

"Come on, let's go and tell the others."

Pauline and Edna gave them their best wishes, and several of the neighbours toasted them. Mary had to keep looking at her ring to make sure that she wasn't dreaming. She still couldn't believe that the man she loved so much wanted to marry her.

"Will you be my chief bridesmaid Pauline please? And Louise will be a little maid too, and I'll ask Kathy and Clara. Oh Pauline, I can't wait."

"I'd love to Mary, and thanks for having Louise too. She will be so excited. Just think, you will be my sister in law."

"Where's Clara?" Mary asked looking around for her friend. I can't wait to ask her, and to show her my ring."

"I couldn't get her to come out Mary. I think she's a bit down, waiting for Graham to come home."

Ron didn't think it right that she should be alone, and went to try and persuade her to come out. He only had to tell her that Mary had something special to ask her, and she agreed. Curiosity got the better of her. She was over the moon for Ron and Mary, and told them that she would love to be one of their bridesmaids.

16

Instead of things being taken off of rationing, it seemed to folks that the government would never let them be free of it. Instead of the happy days everyone had been looking forward to, there was gloom and misery. Men had come home to no work available, due to the business men having to rebuild everything that they had lost in the war days, and others couldn't work because of war wounds, or mental illnesses. A lot of women were now the strongest in the household, and the men weren't too keen on that. It made them feel inadequate and weak, and secretly, they envied the women. Many turned to drink to forget their status in life. One man was even heard to say, that the lucky buggers were the ones that had died, and yet, he must have known that wasn't true.

Edna had expected this to be the norm after the war. It was just the same after the last one. There wasn't the provisions to feed the men what they needed to keep them strong, and the ones that spent all day in the local pubs, were too drunk to help out. One of the neighbours had told Edna.

"I wish he'd never bloody come back. He hardly gives me a penny, and when he does decide to come home, he can hardly stand for the drink he's put down his throat, yet he can always manage to roll his fat belly on top of me, and when he's done, he rolls off again, and falls fast asleep." She carried on calling him. "I tell you what Edna, if I had somewhere to go, I'd bugger off quick and no mistake. I can't go to me Mam's because she tells me that I have to put up with it. She reckons they're all the same."

Things'll get better," Edna tried to reassure her. They have been through a rough time and now they feel useless and bored. They must wonder if it was all worth it.

"I hope you're right Edna, because I can't take much more of this."

Edna sympathised with her. Life could be very cruel, and until things improved, there was nothing that anyone could do. She had been very lucky compared to others. Ron was lucky because he had a job waiting for him, and Pauline had begun her own dressmaking business which was growing rapidly. Both Ron and Mary had been able to save towards the wedding which was booked up for the third Saturday in July. It was to be a small affair with a few family and friends. Edna had managed to swap some of her food rations, for clothing coupons to put towards material for Mary's dress, which Pauline had offered to make for her. She was also to make the bridesmaid dresses so that there would be less money to pay out. Louise's dress was made of parachute silk, that a friend had given to them, and Pauline had dyed it a beautiful tangerine colour.

Clara had received a message from Graham to say that he would be home very soon. He had been sent to a hospital to be cared for until he had got his strength back. It seemed everyone was coming home, but Don.

17

It was a beautiful day for the wedding. The sky was clear of clouds, and the sun was beginning to poke it's head out when Mary awoke. It was as if it had known that today was a special day, for it had been raining heavily over the past two weeks. Feeling both nervous and excited about being Mrs Ronald Adams, Mary was afraid to eat any breakfast, for fear of bringing it back up. Instead, she sat and drank a cup of tea, and ate a homemade biscuit. The wedding wasn't until twelve, and it was now only eight, but Kathy was coming to do her make up, and Pauline, Louise, and Clara would be arriving soon, so that they could all go to the hairdressers together. Afterwards, they were to go to Edna's to get dressed. Ron had gone to sleep at his friend Dave's house because he was to be his best man.

Mary's mother and father, had arrived the night before, and Mrs. Gray had let them have one of her rooms to sleep in. Hearing her mother walking about, Mary guessed that she would soon be in to see her, and it was only seconds after, that she had a knock on her door.

"Can I come in Mary?"

"Yes Mam, of course you can. Is Dad still asleep?"

"Out for the count love. That bed was very comfortable, but I couldn't sleep much for thinking about the wedding."

"Me too. I hope it all goes well."

"Oh it will. Don't start worrying about things like that, there's a good girl. I wonder if Ron's awake yet?"

"I shouldn't think so. He was out with his mates last night. I told him not to drink too much, but you know what they"re like when they all get together."

Her mother laughed, as she well remembered her own wedding. "Your dad could hardly stand still in church, because his mates had poured too much ale down him, and as soon as the vows were over, he had to run for the toilet. He'd said he'd thought he'd have to do it all over the church floor, and was willing the vicar to hurry up."

Mary laughed. "I hope Ron goes then before he goes into church. I'd hate him to have his photo taken with his legs crossed."

"Your dad couldn't wait to have his photo taken. I reckon he'd have had a wet patch if he hadn't gone when he did!" Then she added, "When I've had something to eat, I'll go and see if there is anything I can do to help Edna. She said if the weather was good, she'd put the tables and chairs outside in the garden. That would be nice wouldn't it?"

"Yes, and she also said that they would put Pauline's record player out as well, so that we could have a dance. It'll save them all messing the house up, and if drinks get spilt, it won't ruin her floor."

"I'll take these bottles of sherry I bought."

"Oh Mum, I can't believe I'll soon be Ron's wife. It seems so unreal."

"You'll find out how real it is my dear when you have to spend hours in a queue for a loaf of bread, or some meat. You want to keep well in with your butcher, then if no one is looking, he'll probably put you in an extra sausage, or a bit of offal. You'll be grateful for anything, Remember to always give him a big smile. I've often seen his mates passed a newspaper parcel from under the counter, and we all know what's in it. I'll just say that his mates are better fed than the rest of us."

The conversation came to a halt, when there was a knock on Mrs Gray's front door and Mary shouted. It's ok I'll get it."

"Thanks Mary. Leave the catch off so that they don't have to knock love. It's more than likely there"ll be friends of yours."

"Ok! Will do." And Mary came back carrying a large box of bouquet's and single roses for the button holes.

"Can I see please?"

"Of course you can Mrs Gray."

And when they were shown, Mrs Gray gasped. "Oh Mary, they are beautiful. I've never seen orange roses as nice as that before, and with the trailing leaves, they look so lovely. They really have done you proud haven't they?"

"They certainly have, and I'll be letting them know afterwards. They look so fresh don't they?"

"As if they'd just been picked."

Mary's mother was also impressed, and when she saw the tiny halo of rose buds meant for Louise's head, she reckoned that she'd look a picture in it. Amongst the roses were threaded white gypsophila which made a good contrast. Mary saw the tears welling up in her mother's eyes, and Mary had to beg her not to cry for fear of setting her off as well.

"Hello! Anyone in?"

Edna was about to take the curlers out of her hair when Mary's Mother called her.

Come in, the door's open. I'm only doing my hair so that it's not too tight. I thought it might drop a bit before I have to get dressed. My hat will hide a lot of it, and I don't want to look as though I've got no hair."

"Would you like me to comb it out for you."

"Yes please if you don't mind. Yours always look nice. Is it natural?"

"Yes, but I wouldn't envy it too much if I were you. It has a mind of its own, and won't always go the way I want it to."

"Well I wouldn't mind having it, and that's for sure. I thought I'd have to go to church with no teeth, because I dropped them on the floor when I was getting them out of soak. Me heart went in me mouth. I really thought I'd cracked them, but they were all right, thank the Lord. Can you imagine me all dressed in me Sunday best, and no teeth? I swear Peggy, I'd never have gone to the wedding without them."

Peggy burst out laughing, but Edna looked so serious that she had to apologise to her. "I'm sorry Edna but it sounded so funny." Luckily, Louise came running into the room, and the conversation was changed. "Hello Louise. Are you going to look beautiful today in you lovely dress mummy has made you?"

Louise skipped about happily, nodding her head at the same time, until Pauline came to fetch her for a bath.

"She is such a lovely little girl Edna, and so pretty. I can't wait to see her in her dress. It's going to be a lovely wedding isn't it? What a shame her daddy can't see her. I would think that he would feel very proud. Has Pauline heard from him at all?"

"No, and I don't think she ever will, but you can't tell her that. She has her own ideas and nothing will change them."

"Perhaps it would be a blessing if she didn't. I mean how would you feel having a black man come into your house?"

Edna's nostrils began to flare. Who did this woman think she was? Talk about snobbery! "I'd feel very pleased to have him come Peggy, after all he is Louise's father, and she has a right to see him."

Seeing how much she had upset Edna, Peggy tried to make amends. "Naturally Edna, I didn't mean…."

"I know exactly what you meant Peggy, so don't try to wheedle out of it."

"I'm sorry Edna if I offended you. Please forgive me?"

"We'll say no more about it. I expect there'll be many more say the same thing, but since our Louise has been born, I've changed my own way of thinking."

"I'm off now Mam to Mary's. Is there anything you need doing before I go?" Pauline asked popping her head around the door.

"No, you go love. It'll take the hairdresser a bit of time to do all the hairs. Peggy's offered to help, and we can get it all done whilst Louise's out of the way. We can get the food ready and leave it in the pantry until the last minute."

Arriving home from the hairdressers chattering like a tree full of sparrows, the girls all went into Pauline's to get dressed. Edna and Peggy were pinning their button holes onto the lapels of their jacket and coat. Edna was wearing a matching turquoise dress and coat, and Peggy had on a skirt suit in a magenta colour. John was to wear a black coat and tails, with a tangerine and black patterned cravat. They had hired the suit from a shop in town, but Peggy had bought the cravat to go with it. It wasn't easy finding one with just the right colours in it, but eventually, she had found one on a market stall. Mary was their only daughter, and John was feeling very proud to be walking her up the isle.

Edna watched Louise whilst Pauline and the other girls were getting ready, and when Pauline shouted, "Ok Mam!" She took her to the bedroom for Pauline to dress her. Seeing Mary in her dress, Edna shed a few tears, and so did Peggy when she went to see.

"What a beautiful picture you all make," Edna said, wiping her eyes, and to Mary she said, "Ron will be so proud of you love."

Mary's dress was made of white satin, which had long sleeves that came to a point over the back of her hands, and her headdress was in white lace, which was held into place by pale lemon rose buds. The veil itself, was very long at the back, which had to be carried by the bridesmaids when she walked. Pauline, Clara and Kathy had matching dresses in pale yellow satin, each had a sweetheart neckline, edged with miniature silk tangerine roses which matched Louise's dress exactly. The hems were frilled, and the same rose buds were sewn evenly around. Everyone looked stunning, and when Louise had her dress on, she looked absolutely beautiful. Her dark skin glowed against the tangerine colour of her dress, and her hair hanging in ringlets, held her halo safely. Pauline had given her the basket of matching roses to hold, which she clung tightly on to. Her eyes shone brightly, and in them, Pauline had seen the look of Don which had made her heart ache for him. "I wish that you could see your daughter now," she whispered as she put the finishing touches to her daughter.

After the mother's had been taken to the church, the car came back for the bridesmaids, and then returned for Mary and John. It wasn't far to the church, only a matter of a five minute journey. The front of the church faced towards an open space from which on one side was a park, and to the other, a large house, with a grand gate and doorway. Not only were there relatives waiting to see the bride, but a host of neighbours too, all shouting good luck to Mary as she stepped from the car.

Ron and Dave had arrived earlier, and they had smoked quite a few cigarettes before going into the church. Inside, the church was already packed with well wishers, and Ron and Dave made their way to the pew on the front row to wait for the vicar to nod to them that the bride had arrived, and then, standing at the alter, they stood to attention until the organ began to play the wedding march. Ron couldn't resist a turn of the head to see his bride and her father walking towards them, and his racing heart was in overdrive as he felt the overwhelming love he had for her.

They managed to get through the ceremony, without a fault, and when they were asked to follow to the vestry to sign the licence, one of Edna's friends stood in the pulpit to sing "Ave Maria."

Leaving the church, they had confetti thrown over them, and Mary's hand gripped at covered cardboard horseshoes that she had been handed. Edna gave Louise a wooden spoon trimmed with lemon ribbon to give to Mary, and going up to her, she tugged at Mary's dress to be noticed. Mary bent down to kiss her, just as the photographer was taking a photograph, and seeing what a good picture it would make, he asked Mary and Ron to bend again to Louise's level so that he could snap them. After that, he took several more photographs of the bride and groom alone, and with the bridesmaids, and the final one, he took of all the families together.

The meal went down a treat, and many of the guests commented on its flavour. The salad had been picked fresh from the garden before being prepared, and Ron had managed to get some pork and pies from one of the men on the black market racket. It had cost him two days pay, but he was grateful to get it. He'd managed to get a few luxury items since being home, but you had to know who to go to to get it. Some of the things were smuggled in from France, but it was best not to ask questions. You just paid your money, and collected what you had paid for.

With the tables moved to one side, Pauline put some records on to the player to dance to. Mary and Ron danced the first dance together, and then others began to join in. Looking down at his bride, Ron told her how lovely she was looking, and how lucky he was to have married her.

"I can't believe that I am now Mrs Adams. Pinch me to see if I am awake." Ron pinched her hard.

"Ouch, not that hard," she told him, laughing.

The afternoon was filled with music, laughter, and singing, but soon it was time for Mary and Ron to leave to catch their train to Cleethorpes where they were to spend their honeymoon. They had found a small terraced house to rent for when they returned, and they had spent every spare time that they could manage doing it all up. They had already got a few pieces of furniture that was given to them, and Ron had managed to get some cheap paint, to decorate it. Mary liked the long garden it had. She said it would be nice for their children to play in, where as Ron had laughed, and asked how many she was thinking of having. Oh lots, she had replied, and Ron had taken her into his arms, and told her. "I guess we'll have to start making them as soon as we are married." And Mary had blushed.

They said their goodbyes to their guests, and were about to get into the taxi which was waiting to take them to the station, when another one turned up behind the first car. Thinking there had been some mistake, Ron walked over to the second car to speak to the driver, but when he poked his head through the open window, he got the shock of his life, for there was Graham with a big grin on his face, about to step out.

"Don't tell me I've missed it all," he said laughing. "Trust old Graham to be late. Is there any food left? I'm starving."

"Plenty mate. It's good to see you." And Ron shouted to Mary to come and see.

"Graham! Oh Clara is going to be so happy to see you. They are all in the garden. Go on in. I'm sorry we have to leave now."

"That's alright, you don't want to miss your first night together do you?" Again, Mary blushed, but Graham offered them his best wishes, and said that he hoped his own wedding would be very soon.

Instead of going straight into the garden, Graham stood at the gate trying to see if he could find Clara amongst the rest of the crowd. He finally saw her dancing the jitterbug with Kathy, and walked up behind them, tapped Clara on the shoulder, and said, "My dance I believe."

Clara couldn't believe her ears, and when she looked at him, all she could do was to burst into tears.

"Hey! I'm not that ugly am I?"

Between sobs, Clara asked him when he arrived home.

"This afternoon. I dropped my bags off at home and came straight here. Now, are we going to have that dance or what?"

Pauline had seen him come into the garden and was watching the reaction of Clara, and then she changed the record for a slow waltz for them to dance to. Secretly, she felt like crying herself, as she wished that it was Don instead.

There were many people with tears in their eyes when they saw how happy the young couple were as they danced together. It was obvious that they were both very much in love. When the dance was over, graham whispered something into Clara's ear, and she nodded to him. He then walked over to Pauline and asked her to dance with him. As they danced, he told her.

"Pauline, I have something very important to tell you. Can we go somewhere quiet?"

Intrigued, Pauline took him into the house, and into the lounge.

"What is it Graham? If it's about making Clara's wedding dress, I've already said that I will make it."

"It's not that Pauline, it's about your feller, Don."

Pauline's heart skipped a beat. "What about him Graham? Is he hurt? How did you get to find out about him?"

"He was in the same prisoner of war camp that I was in. He's been through a really rough time Pauline. It's going to take a lot of help for him to get better, if he ever does. I don't know what caused it, but whatever it was, it's left him in a pretty bad way."

"I want to see him Graham. Where is he? Tell me where he is, and I'll go to him."

"You can't, not yet Pauline. He's been sent to a hospital in America, but I've got an address for you to write to him."

"Oh Graham, I love yer. Thanks for that." And she planted a kiss onto his cheek, just as Clara and Kathy walked in, and

105

jumping up, she flung her arms around them and said, "It's such wonderful news about Don isn't it? You do know don't yer?"

"We do. Graham told me whilst we were dancing, and we're both thrilled for you Pauline. It's been a good day all round hasn't it?" Pauline nodded in agreement, before running out to tell her Mam her news.

Edna was pleased for her daughter, it had been a long time since she had seen Pauline look so happy.

Pauline couldn't wait to write her letter, and excused herself so that she could go to her bedroom to begin it.

My darling Don.

Graham has just given me the news about you, and where you are. I still can't believe that I am writing this letter. I have missed you so much my darling, but I have never given up hope of you returning to me. You must get well soon, for I can't wait to see you again. I shall pray for you every night, and God willing, he will give you all the help that you need to recover.

I have the most precious gift for you, and I know that you will love her as much as I do. Her name is Louise, but I call her button nose, because she has the most cutest of noses you have ever seen. Yes my darling, she is your daughter, and she is so looking forward to meeting her daddy for the first time. I have told her how much I love you, and how much she looks like you. She has your beautiful eyes Don, and when I look into them, I see you, and my heart pounds for the love that I hold for you.

I have been told many times that you will not come back to me, but our love was too great, and I know that one day you will.

Ron and Mary were married today, and Louise and I were bridesmaids. I will send you a photograph as soon as I have one.

Until I see you again my love, please put all your effort into getting well for us both, so that I can hold you in my arms again.

My endless love to you.

-Pauline. XX

It was three weeks, before she had a reply. It wasn't from Don, but a nurse at the hospital where he was a patient.

Dear Miss Adams,

I am replying to your letter on behalf of Mr Donald Smith, who unfortunately is unable to reply himself.

I think he was pleased to hear from you, as there was a slight improvement of his illness afterwards. Naturally I can't say if Mr Smith will recover fully, but if you could keep writing to him, then I am hoping that it will be some help towards some sort of a recovery. Thank you for reading my letter.

Yours faithfully

-Nurse Jackson.

Pauline showed it to Edna, who said how kind of the nurse to bother like that. "Perhaps your letters might be of help Pauline. You can only try love."

"I'll write every day Mam, and I'll keep my fingers crossed that they do."

"And me too Pauline."

Pauline did mail to Don every day, and when she at last had a photograph of Louise, she asked her to put a kiss on the back of it. Louise didn't think one would be enough, and covered the whole back in them instead.

Smiling, Pauline put it into an envelope, and took Louise to the post box with her to post it.

Recognising the handwriting, Nurse Jackson hurried to Don's bedside.

"Another letter for you," she told him, handing it over to him. "Would you like me to read it to you?"

Don didn't answer, but as she usually did, she tore open the envelope ready to begin reading, but as she opened the letter, something fell out and landed on to Don's bed. She was about to pick it up, when Don's hand got there first. This was something special for the nurse, because any other time he would have ignored it. She delayed reading the letter, and watched him instead as he looked at the photograph. At first he only held it, but after a while, he began to look at it. His nurse wondered if anything was registering in his mind, and she longed him to give some reaction. Suddenly, he turned over the photograph, and then holding it close to his cheek, he began to cry. Softly at first, and then louder and louder, as all of the hurt in his body was being released.

"That's it, let it out," his nurse told him. This was a very good sign and she felt that now, they would gain some headway towards him being well again. There were many men on the ward like Donald, and she knew from experience that crying was a good sign. Instead of reading his letter, she left him to cry in private. Men didn't like to be seen crying, and she would give him time to empty his emotions completely.

Nurse Jackson wasn't on duty the next day, but even though she was away from the hospital, she still wondered how her patient was doing, and the following day, she couldn't wait to see him. Going to his bed, she saw an entirely different man, because Don was sitting, held up with pillows, and the photograph was on the cupboard at the side of him.

"My! You are beginning to look better," she told him, straightening his bed a little.

"My daughter," he told her, showing her the photograph.

"That is easy to see, for she has your eyes. She is beautiful."

"I'd like to write to her please, if you have a pen and some paper."

"I'll fetch you some, but don't write too much just yet. We don't want you overdoing it."

"Thank you. I won't."

He began to write:

My adorable daughter Louise,
Thank you for sending me the photograph. Daddy will be home to see you one day, and we will all live together. I love you very much. Give your mummy a kiss from me.
All my love Daddy. Xxxxxxxxxx

He also wrote to Pauline:

Pauline my darling,
Please forgive me for not being there for you. I will explain everything when I see you. Thank you for writing to me, I have all of your letters, and I am sorry that I have only just been able to reply to you myself. I am being well looked after in here, and when I am truly recovered, I shall keep my promise to you my darling, and shall come to marry you, if you will still have me."

Take care my precious one. I love you dearly. -Don. xx

18

With only one week to go before Christmas Day, Pauline and Edna had been hiding presents from Louise. It would be even better this year, as Louise was old enough to get excited, and she had been making paper chains from crepe paper that Pauline had cut into strips. It was fair to say, that there was more glue on her apron, than was on the chains, but she was enjoying making them. Every now and again, Pauline would here the sound of a sigh, as some of the chains split, and she couldn't help smiling. Louise was so engrossed in what she was doing and her little tongue was sticking out of the corner of her mouth as she concentrated. The week before, Edna had taken her to see Father Christmas at Lewis's department store, and her eyes had lit up at the sight of the mechanical elves hammering away at toys, whilst little fairies flew overhead.

"Pauline when have you to pick up that D.O.L.L.Y.?" Edna spelt it out so that Louise didn't hear.

"In the morning Mam, would yer have Louise whilst I go? I shouldn't be long."

"Of course I will. You don't have to ask. We'll put the tree up, she'll enjoy that."

"Do yer hear that Louise, Nanna's going to put the Christmas tree up tomorrer. Are yer going to help her?"

"Yes!" Louise shouted, clapping her hands with excitement making Edna laugh.

"I've got some milk bottle tops. If I fetch them, would you like to make some little bells? I've got a marble you can shape them over, but you mustn't put the marble in your mouth or you might swallow it," Edna told her.

"I won't Nan, I'm big now aren't I?"

"You certainly are love."

Pauline could hardly contain her own excitement. "I can't wait, can you Mam? I'm longing to see her face Christmas morning."

"It is nice to have a child in the house at this time of year. Ron and Mary want to come around early to see her open her presents. I've told them that they might as well stay for dinner with us."

"It's been a good year mam, hasn't it?"

"Much better than I expected Pauline, that's for sure."

"I wish Don was well enough to come and see her."

"If he can't make it this year, there'll always be next year love."

"I know, but that's a long time off."

"Believe me, it will fly by Pauline. So fast that you will wonder where the year has gone."

That evening when Louise was in bed, they wrapped up the presents that they had already bought. Pauline had potato stamped over some tissue paper to use for wrapping, and she had tied some ribbon around them to make them look pretty.

It had seemed a very long week, but eventually Christmas Eve arrived, and Edna was busy preparing the potatoes and Brussel sprouts for dinner the next day. She had got a small chicken from the farm up the road, and had washed and cleaned it fully. She had managed to make a little basin of stuffing, but that wouldn't be put into the bird until the very last minute. Louise had been put into bed in the afternoon for a sleep, so that she could be taken to the Town Hall that evening to hear the choir sing carols.

Mary and Ron arrived at five o'clock, and handed Pauline a sack of presents to be put under the tree before going to bed, and Pauline quickly put them into a cupboard to hide them.

"Uncle Ron, Santa's coming tonight!" Louise called to her uncle.

"I know, and I've hung up my stocking all ready for him to fill it." Louise then ran to fetch her stocking to show him. "That's a nice big one. Santa will need a big sleigh this year won't he?

"Yes," replied Louise, and then she asked, "Are you coming to see the singers with us?"

"We are love, and I can't wait."

"It's great having a child in the house at this time of the year Mary," Pauline told her friend. "Yer should hurry up an' have one before next Christmas."

"I agree Pauline, and that's what we intend to do, and so we thought if we had it in June, then he or she might be able to join in some of the fun with the rest of us."

Pauline began to count. "Hold on a minute, yer do realise that…." And then she managed to take on board what Mary was saying to her. "Yer mean?"

"Yes, isn't it wonderful?"

"It's great! Hear that Louise? Yer going to have a little cousin to play with."

"When?"

"Soon love. Not quite yet, yer'll have to wait for a bit longer."

Edna was thrilled, and told them so, and getting out the sherry, she said, "This calls for a drink," and poured them all one each.

Louise, dressed in a red velvet coat and bonnet, and wearing long black boots on her feet, ran down the tram to find a seat, and then she plonked herself down on it, making room for her Mum and Gran. Ron and Mary sat down to face them.

"Can we sing tonight Mummy?"

"Yes love yer certainly can, and we all want to hear yer."

The town hall square was lit up with fairy lights, and Louise couldn't speak, she was so enthralled. Having to bend her head backwards to see the top of the Christmas tree, almost made her fall, but Ron picked her up so that she could see better, and when the choir came out to sing, he sat her onto his shoulder's, so that she could have a good view of them, and she sang her little heart out. Pauline hoped that it would be a memory that would stay with her daughter for a very long time. Realising that she had suddenly stopped singing, Pauline looked up to find Louise fast asleep, with her head dropped over onto Ron's. She whispered to Ron, and he lifted her down to carry her in his arms. She was still asleep when they arrived home, and Pauline took off her boots and clothes gently, and lay her inside her cot for the night.

Pauline was awake first, but she didn't wake Louise. Instead, she crept down the stairs to light a fire, and make her Mam a cup of tea. Ron and Mary, said that they would arrive about eight, so it was best that Louise got as much sleep as possible, but Ron had other ideas as it was only seven thirty when they turned up.

"This is a funny eight o'clock," Pauline told them.

"I know, we couldn't wait. Give me that tea, and I'll take it up to Mam for you. Where's Louise? We thought she'd have been up early."

"Still asleep. I think last night really wore her out."

"We can't have that on a Christmas morning can we? Shall I wake her?"

"I can see there'll be no stopping yer." And when Ron walked up the stairs singing "Away in a Manger," Pauline heard Louise shout out, "Uncle Ron!" And when he returned, he was carrying Louise.

"Look what Santa left me," he said, bouncing Louise up and down.

"Santa not," Louise replied laughing, but when she saw the presents beneath the tree, she begged him. "Down, me down." And when he put her onto the floor, she ran to grab them.

"Steady love, and mummy will pass yer yours. We have to wait for Nan."

"It's alright Pauline, I'm up." And Edna came to sit by the fire to get warm, whilst Pauline passed around the presents, making sure that Louise got two to their one, but when she opened her dolly, she wanted to play with it, until Ron gave her his and Mary's. He had made her a doll's house, which he had painted white with a red roof. Mary had made some furniture from empty match boxes, and also a tiny doll from pipe cleaners. Louise loved it instantly, and began to move around the furniture.

"That's lovely both of yer," Pauline told them. "Yer both very good to her."

A knock came at the door just then, and Pauline ran to open it. "It'll be Graham and Clara!" she shouted out to the others. Opening the door, but all she could see, was a large pile of presents.

"Ho! Ho! Ho! Merry Christmas!" Graham bellowed out, popping his head around the door. I've brought you a big present."

"Come out, come out whoever yer are!" Pauline shouted laughing at the same time, and waited for Clara to poke her head out, but instead of Clara, Pauline got the shock of her life, for in front of her, stood Don.

Unable to move, she stood there gaping at him.

"Well, aren't you going to invite him in?" And Graham left them to be alone.

"I'm sorry love. I just can't believe that it's you. If yer knew how many times I'd wished for this day." And she pulled him towards her crying. Putting his gifts down, Don took her up into his arms and kissed her passionately.

"Oh my darling, I owe you such an explanation." And he related how he'd been sent abroad to avoid him marrying her. "There was no way I could let you know at the time, but I hoped that you knew that I hadn't done it deliberately."

"Never for one minute. I knew that yer'd come eventually. I trusted yer not to let me down, an' yer haven't.

"Who is it Pauline? You're letting in a draught."

"Sorry Mam, I'll close the door." And then she took Don to meet her mother. I've got the best present ever Mam, my Don has come back to me."

Ron was the first to shake his hand, and welcome him, and then Edna told him to sit down, and make himself at home. She was overwhelmed with happiness for her Pauline.

Pauline bent down to Louise, who was still playing. "Louise, Santa has bought yer a very special present, would yer like to see it?" Nodding, Louise stood up, and Pauline took her over to Don. "Look sweetheart, this is yer daddy."

Louise became very shy, and ran over to Edna to hide her face, until Edna told her. "Go and say hello to him Louise. He's come a long way to see you."

Slowly, Louise began to make her way towards him, and Don knelt onto the floor with his arms open, until Louise reached him, and he hugged her tightly to him. "Hello Louise," he said with eyes watering. I've come home to you and your mummy. Look I have your photograph that you sent me." And he took it from his wallet to show her.

"That's my pretty dress," she said pointing.

"Yes and that's my pretty daughter," Don told her, pointing at her photograph. Louise laughed. After Don had given presents to everyone, including a large teddy bear for Louise, she sat on his knee as if she had known him for all of her life.

When she did get down, Don asked Edna if she would mind him speaking to Pauline in private, and Edna told them to use the front room, where Don went onto one knee to propose. "Pauline Adams, would you do me the honour of marrying me?" And opening up a tiny box, he took out a diamond ring for her finger. Pauline didn't need to be asked twice, and held out her hand for him to put the ring on, just managing to squeeze out a yes, because she was crying too much. Before going back to tell her family their news, Don told her again how much he loved her, and kissed her.

Edna had guessed what he had wanted, but pretended to be surprised as well as pleased, and again the sherry was poured out. Louise couldn't stop looking at the ring, it sparkled so much from the light, and when Don picked her up. Pauline looked into their eyes, and said a silent thank you, thinking that this was her best Christmas ever, whilst Edna was thinking of how she had almost ruined Pauline's happiness. Ron was looking at Mary, and thinking that this time next year, they would have a child of their own to spoil. You never knew what was around the corner waiting for you! This year had proved that much, and holding up their glasses, they made a toast to 1946.

Printed in the United States
60062LVS00002B/7-54

9 781424 132195